THE EARTH IS THE LORD'S

The Earth Is the Lord's

Essays on Stewardship

Edited by
Mary Evelyn Jegen
Executive Director,
Bread for the World Educational Fund
and
Bruno Manno
Director, Office for Moral and Religious Education,
University of Dayton

PAULIST PRESS
New York/Ramsey/Toronto

Copyright © 1978 by
The Missionary Society
of St. Paul the Apostle
in the State of New York

Library of Congress
Catalog Card Number: 77-83588

ISBN: 0-8091-2067-4

Published by Paulist Press
Editorial Office: 1865 Broadway, New York, N.Y. 10023
Business Office: 545 Island Road, Ramsey, N.J. 07446

Printed and bound in the
United States of America

Contents

v

III

RESPONSES

Foreword

Today, one out of every eight human beings suffers degrading and destructive hunger. Christians dare not rest easy in the face of such suffering. They cannot forget the words of their Lord, "I tell you solemnly, insofar as you did this to one of the least of these brothers of mine, you did it to me."

Hunger will likely remain a central human issue for at least the remainder of this century. Most have by now learned that traditional individual response to world hunger, no matter how generous and well intentioned, is simply inadequate to the size and complexity of the problem. That is why *Bread for the World*, a Christian citizens' movement, advocates U.S. government policies which address the basic causes of hunger. Three years of consistent effort have taught *Bread for the World* that there are no quick or simple political solutions to the hunger problem. Years of painstaking effort at issue analysis and citizen action lie ahead before all people in this country and throughout the world will be able to exercise their God-given right to a nutritionally adequate diet. Yet the goal is in sight, according to the National Academy of Sciences, which reported in June 1977 to President Carter, "If there is the political will in this country and abroad . . . it would be possible to overcome the worst aspects of widespread hunger and malnutrition within a generation."

Fostering the political will necessary to keep faith with the hungry of the world is perhaps the greatest single challenge we face. For this reason, *Bread for the World Educational Fund* has embarked on a long-range educational program, *Decade of Commitment on World Hunger,* in collaboration with a growing number of colleges, universities, and theological seminaries.

As part of this program, in November 1976, *Bread for the World Educational Fund* and the University of Dayton through its Office for Moral and Religious Education co-sponsored a seminar on "Stewardship: A Christian Perspective on Ownership and Use of Essential Resources." The purpose was to search our Christian tradition regarding the goods of the earth, and to relate that tradition to world hunger. The essays in this volume are the fruit of that seminar.

If there is one idea that underlies all the essays, it is that we must learn to make decisions about food on the basis of all people's human rights and basic needs. No matter how much human effort is involved in the production, processing, distribution and preparation of what we eat, food remains basically the gift of a gracious Creator. It is a gift intended for all people, a gift that we hold in trust, along with the land and all the bountiful resources of the earth.

What difference would it make to the hungry of the world if this Judaeo-Christian tradition of "holding in trust" were the prevailing notion guiding our social practices and our political policies? This is a crucial question if we are to learn to see the world hunger problem as an issue of social justice, rather than one simply of economics or technology. The essays in this book probe some of the implications of that question.

The first part of the book explores our biblical, theological, and philosophical tradition on stewardship in order to challenge common secular assumptions about property rights, competition, and equity. There follows a set of essays laying out a complex range of issues that need rethinking and new solutions. Finally, there are reflections of several persons whose personal and family lives have been consciously influenced and transformed by the psalmist's words, "The earth is the Lord's."

Whether we like it or not, the consequences of our actions and inactions are felt throughout the world by millions of people we will never know. A basic argument of *Bread for the World* is that our political response to world hunger is essential. Government policies may multiply or nullify a hundredfold all private efforts, however generous, to help hungry people. Readers of these essays should come away with a clearer understanding why this thesis is true.

We are called to be stewards of all our gifts. Certainly among the most precious is our citizenship in a free society, which carries with it the power to help shape public policy. To neglect the stewardship of this gift of political power is to fail in a sacred trust.

The opinions in these essays are those of the authors and do not represent an official position of *Bread for the World Educational Fund* or the Office for Moral and Religious Education of the University of Dayton. The collection is offered as a service to the growing number of Christians meeting in groups, large and small, to study the issue of hunger. If the book helps readers see more clearly the link between their Christian faith and their responsibility as stewards in a land of power and plenty, it will have achieved its purpose.

Eugene Carson Blake,
President, *Bread for the World*

I
Perspectives

A Biblical Perspective on Stewardship

Ronald J. Sider

This essay develops two biblical themes.[1] First, the God of Scripture is not a neutral observer of struggles for justice; rather he is actively at work in history on the side of the poor. Second, God wills transformed economic relationships among his people "that there may be equality" (2 Cor. 8:14).

I
GOD IS ON THE SIDE OF THE POOR

The Central Points of Revelation History

The Exodus. God displayed his power at the exodus in order to free oppressed slaves. When God called Moses at the burning bush, he informed Moses that his intention was to end suffering and injustice (Ex. 3:7-8; also 6:5ff). Each year at the harvest festival, the Israelites repeated a liturgical confession celebrating the way God had acted to free a poor, oppressed people.

> A wandering Aramean was my father; and he went down into Egypt and sojourned there. . . . And the Egyptians treated us harshly and afflicted us, and laid upon us hard bondage. Then we cried to the Lord, the God of our fathers, and the Lord heard our voice, and saw our affliction, our toil, and our oppression; and the Lord brought us out of Egypt with a mighty hand (Deut. 26:5ff).

The God of the Bible cares when people enslave and oppress

1

others. At the exodus he acted to end economic oppression and bring freedom to slaves.

Before Yahweh gave the two tables of the Law, he identified himself: "I am the Lord your God who brought you out of the land of Egypt, out of the house of bondage" (Deut. 5:6; Ex. 20:2). Yahweh is the one who frees from bondage. The God of the Bible wants to be known as the liberator of the oppressed.

The exodus was certainly the decisive event in the creation of the chosen people. We distort the biblical interpretation of this momentous occasion unless we see that, at this pivotal point, the Lord of the universe was at work correcting oppression and liberating the poor.

Destruction of the Nation and Captivity. When they settled in the promised land, the Israelites soon discovered that Yahweh's passion for justice was a two-edged sword. When they were oppressed, it led to their freedom. But when they became the oppressors, it led to their destruction.

When God called Israel out of Egypt and made his covenant with them, he gave them his Law so that they could live together in peace and justice. But Israel failed to obey the Law of the covenant. As a result, God destroyed Israel and sent his chosen people into captivity. Why? The explosive message of the prophets is that God destroyed Israel because of mistreatment of the poor.

The middle of the eighth century B.C. was a time of political success and economic prosperity unknown since the days of Solomon. But it was precisely at this moment that God sent his prophet Amos to announce the unwelcome news that the northern kingdom would be destroyed. Why? Penetrating beneath the facade of current prosperity and fantastic economic growth, Amos saw terrible oppression of the poor. He saw the rich "trample the head of the poor into the dust of the earth" (2:7). He saw that the affluent life-style of the rich was built on oppression of the poor (6:1-7). He denounced the rich women ("cows" was Amos' word) "who oppress the poor, who crush the needy, who say to their husbands, 'Bring that we may drink!'" Even in the courts the poor had no hope because the rich bribed the judges (5:10-15).

God's word through Amos was that the northern kingdom would be destroyed and the people taken into exile (7:11, 17).

Woe to those who lie upon beds of ivory and stretch themselves upon their couches and eat lambs from the flock and calves from the midst of the stall. . . . Therefore, they shall now be the first of those to go into exile, and the revelry of those who stretch themselves shall pass away (6:4-7).

Only a very few years after Amos spoke, it happened just as God had said. The Assyrians conquered the northern kingdom and took thousands into captivity. Because of their mistreatment of the poor, God destroyed the northern kingdom—forever.

God sent other prophets to announce the same fate for the southern kingdom of Judah (cf. Is. 10:1-4; Mi. 2:2; 3:12). But they continued to oppress the poor and helpless. As a result, Jeremiah declared that God would use the Babylonians to destroy Judah (Jer. 5:26-31; 7:5-6). In 587 B.C., Jerusalem fell and the Babylonian captivity began.

God destroyed Israel and Judah because of their mistreatment of the poor. The cataclysmic catastrophe of national destruction and captivity reveals the God of the exodus still at work correcting the oppression of the poor.

The Incarnation. Christians believe that God revealed himself most completely in Jesus of Nazareth. How did the Incarnate One define his mission?

His words in the synagogue at Nazareth, spoken near the beginning of his public ministry, still throb with hope for the poor. He read from the prophet Isaiah:

The Spirit of the Lord is upon me, because he has anointed me to preach good news to the poor. He has sent me to proclaim release to the captives and recovery of sight to the blind, to set at liberty those who are oppressed, to proclaim the acceptable year of the Lord (Lk. 4:18-19).

After reading these words, he informed the audience that this Scripture was now fulfilled in himself. The mission of the Incarnate One was to free the oppressed and heal the blind. The poor are the only group specifically singled out as recipients of Jesus' Gospel. Certainly the Gospel Jesus proclaimed was for all, but he was

particularly concerned that the poor realize that his Good News
was for them.[2]

Jesus' actual ministry corresponded to his words in Luke 4.
He spent most of his time, not among the rich and powerful in
Jerusalem, but rather among the poor in the cultural and economic
backwater of Galilee. He healed the sick and blind. He fed the
hungry. And he warned his followers in the strongest possible
words that those who do not feed the hungry, clothe the naked and
visit the prisoners will experience eternal damnation (Mt. 25:31ff).
At the supreme moment of history when God himself took on
human flesh, we see the God of Israel still at work liberating the
poor and oppressed and summoning his people to do the same.

The foundation of Christian concern for the hungry and oppressed is simply that God cares especially for them. He demon-
strated his concern when he freed oppressed slaves at the exodus.
He underlined that concern in an awesome way when he obliter-
ated the nations of Israel and Judah for their economic injustice.
And he expressed that concern most vividly when he became flesh
and walked among us to heal the broken and set at liberty those
who are oppressed. At the pivotal points of God's self-disclosure in
history, he revealed himself as the liberator of the poor.

God Identifies with the Poor

Not only does God act in history to liberate the poor. In a
mysterious way that we can only half fathom, the all-powerful
sovereign of the universe identifies in a special way with the weak
and destitute.

Two powerful proverbs state this beautiful truth. Proverbs
14:31 puts it negatively: "He who oppresses a poor man insults his
Maker." Even more moving is the positive formulation: "He who is
kind to the poor lends to the Lord" (19:17). What a statement!
Helping a poor person is like helping the Creator of all things with a
loan.

Only in the incarnation can we begin dimly to perceive what
God's identification with the weak, oppressed and poor really
means. "Though he was rich," St. Paul says of our Lord Jesus, "yet
for our sake he became poor" (2 Cor. 8:9). Born in a barn, raised a

carpenter, he never owned a home, and died penniless. Yet he was God Incarnate.

Only as we feel the presence of the Incarnate God in the form of a poor Galilean can we begin to understand his words:

> I was hungry and you gave me food, I was thirsty and you gave me drink. . . . I was naked and you clothed me. . . . Truly I say to you, as you did it to one of the least of these my brethren, you did it to me (Mt. 25:35ff).

What does it mean to feed and clothe the Creator of all things? We cannot know. We can only look on the poor and oppressed with new eyes and resolve anew to heal their hurts and help end their oppression.

If his first saying is awesome, the second is terrifying. "Truly I say to you, as you did it not to one of the least of these, you did it not to me" (v. 45). What does that saying mean in a world where millions die each year while rich Christians live in affluence? What does it mean to see the Lord of the universe lying by the roadside starving and walk on the other side? We cannot know. We can only pledge in fear and trembling not to kill him again.

Christian faith is a faith focused on the incarnation. The Incarnate One tells us that God identifies in a special way with the poor.

God Casts Down the Rich and Exalts the Poor

Jesus' story of the rich man and Lazarus echoes a central, biblical teaching. The rich may prosper for a time, but eventually God will destroy them. The poor on the other hand, God will exalt. Mary's Magnificat puts it simply and bluntly:

> My soul magnifies the Lord. . . . He has put down the mighty from their thrones and exalted those of low degree; he has filled the hungry with good things, and the rich he has sent empty away (Lk. 1:46-53).[3]

"Come now, you rich, weep and howl for the miseries that are coming upon you" (Jas. 5:1) is a constant theme of biblical revelation.

Why does Scripture declare that God regularly reverses the good fortunes of the rich? Is God engaged in class warfare? Actually our texts never say that God loves the poor more than the rich. But they constantly assert that God lifts up the poor and disadvantaged, and they persistently assert that God casts down the wealthy and powerful—precisely because they became wealthy by oppressing the poor and because they failed to feed the hungry.

Why did James warn the rich to weep and howl because of impending misery? Because they had cheated their workers: "You have laid up treasure for the last days. Behold the wages of the laborers who mowed your fields, which you kept back by fraud, cry out; and the cries of the harvesters have reached the ears of the Lord of hosts. You have lived on earth in luxury and in pleasure; you have fattened your hearts in a day of slaughter" (5:3-5). God does not have class enemies, but he hates and punishes injustice and neglect of the poor. And the rich, if we accept the repeated warnings of Scripture, are frequently guilty of both.

Long before the days of James, the psalmist and the prophets knew that the rich were often rich because of oppression.

Wicked men are found among my people; they lurk like fowlers lying in wait. They set a trap; they catch men. Like a basket full of birds, their houses are full of treachery; therefore they have become great and rich, they have grown fat and sleek. They know no bounds in deeds of wickedness; they judge not with justice the cause of the fatherless, to make it prosper, and they do not defend the rights of the needy. Shall I not punish them for these things? says the Lord (Jer. 5:26-29).[4]

Nor was the faith of Jeremiah and the psalmist mere wishful thinking. Through his prophets, God announced devastation and destruction for both rich individuals and rich nations who oppressed the poor. And it happened as they had prophesied. Because the rich oppress the poor and weak, the Lord of history is at work pulling down their houses and kingdoms.

Sometimes Scripture does not charge the rich with direct

oppression of the poor. It simply accuses them of failure to share with the needy—but the result is the same. In the story of the rich man and Lazarus (Lk. 16), Jesus does not say that Dives exploited Lazarus. He merely shows that the affluent Dives had no concern for the sick beggar lying outside his gate.

The biblical explanation of Sodom's destruction provides another illustration of this terrible truth. Ezekiel says that one important reason God destroyed Sodom was because she stubbornly refused to share with the poor!

> Behold, this was the guilt of your sister Sodom; she and her daughters had pride, surfeit of food, and prosperous ease, but did not aid the poor and needy. They were haughty, and did abominable things before me; therefore, I removed them when I saw it (Ez. 16:49-50).

The text does not say that they oppressed the poor (although they probably did). It simply accuses them of failing to assist the needy.

The God of the Bible wreaks horrendous havoc on the rich, but it is not because he does not love rich persons. It is because the rich regularly oppress the poor and neglect the needy.

God Commands His People To Have a Special Concern for the Poor

In every strand of biblical literature, we find God commanding believers to have special regard for the poor, weak and disadvantaged.

Equal justice for the poor in court is a constant theme of Scripture. The Torah commanded it (Ex. 23:6). The psalmist invoked divine assistance for the king so that he could provide it (Ps. 72:1-4). And the prophets announced devastating destruction because the rulers stubbornly subverted it (Am. 5:10-15).

Widows, orphans and strangers receive particularly frequent attention (e.g., Ex. 22:21-24). The Bible specifically commands believers to imitate God's special concern for the poor and oppressed (e.g., Ex. 22:21ff; Lk. 6:33ff; 2 Cor. 8:9; 1 Jn. 3:16ff). In fact, it underlines the command by teaching that when God's people care for the poor, they imitate God himself. But that is not all. God's word teaches that those who neglect the poor and oppressed are really not God's people at all—no matter how frequent their religious rituals or how orthodox their creeds and confessions.

Worship in the context of mistreatment of the poor and disadvantaged, God thundered again and again through the prophets, is an outrage. Isaiah denounced Israel (he called her Sodom and Gomorrah) because she tried to worship Yahweh and oppress the weak at the same time:

> Hear the word of the Lord, you rulers of Sodom! Give ear to the teaching of our God, you people of Gomorrah! What to me is the multitude of your sacrifices? . . . Bring no more vain offerings; incense is an abomination to me. New moon and Sabbath and the calling of assemblies—I cannot endure iniquity and solemn assembly. Your new moons and your appointed feasts my soul hates. . . . Even though you make many prayers, I will not listen; your hands are full of blood (Is. 1:10-15).[5]

Nor has God changed. Jesus repeated the same theme. He warned the people about scribes who secretly oppress widows while making a public display of their piety. Their pious looking garments and frequent visits to the synagogue are a sham. Woe to religious hypocrites "who devour widows' houses and for a pretense make long prayers" (Mk. 12:38-40).

The biblical word against religious hypocrites raises an extremely difficult question. Are the people of God truly God's people if they oppress the poor? Is the Church really the Church if it does not work to free the oppressed?

We have seen how God declared through the prophet Isaiah that the people of Israel were really Sodom and Gomorrah rather than the people of God (1:10). God simply could not tolerate their exploitation of the poor and disadvantaged any longer. Jesus was even more blunt and sharp. To those who do not feed the hungry, clothe the naked, and visit the prisoners, he will speak a terrifying word at the final judgment: "Depart from me, you cursed, into the eternal fire prepared for the devil and his angels" (Mt. 25:41). The meaning is clear and unambiguous. Jesus intends his disciples to imitate his own special concern for the poor and needy. Those who disobey will experience eternal damnation.

Lest we forget the warning, God repeats it in 1 John. "But if anyone has the world's goods and sees his brother in need, yet closes his heart against him, how does God's love abide in him? Little children, let us not love in word or speech but in deed and truth (3:17-18). Again, the words are plain. What do they mean for Western Christians who demand increasing affluence each year while fellow Christians in the third world suffer malnutrition, deformed bodies and brains, even starvation? The text clearly says that if we fail to aid the needy, we do not have God's love—no matter how punctilious our piety or how orthodox our doctrine. Regardless of what we do or say at 11:00 Sunday morning, affluent people who neglect the poor are not the people of God.

But still the question persists. Are Church members no longer Christians because of continuing sin? Obviously not. We are members of the people of God not because of our own righteousness but solely because of Christ's death for us.

But that response is inadequate. Matthew 25 and 1 John 3 surely mean more than that the people of God are disobedient (but still justified all the same) when they neglect the poor. These verses pointedly assert that some people so disobey God that they are not his people at all in spite of their pious profession. Neglect of the poor is one of the oft-repeated biblical signs of such disobedience. Certainly none of us would claim that we fulfill Matthew 25 perfectly. And we cling to the hope of forgiveness. But there comes a point—and, thank God, he alone knows where!—when neglect of the poor is no longer forgiven. It is punished. Eternally.

Is it not possible—indeed very probable—that a vast majority of Western Christians have reached that point? Can we seriously claim that we are obeying the biblical command to have a special concern for the poor? Can we seriously claim that we are imitating God's concern for the poor and oppressed? Can we seriously hope to experience eternal love rather than eternal separation from the God of the poor?

God is on the side of the poor! The Bible clearly and re-

peatedly teaches that God is at work in history pulling down the
rich and exalting the poor. At the central points of the history of
revelation, God acted not only to reveal himself, but also to liberate poor, oppressed people.

God actively opposes the rich since they neglect or oppose
justice because justice demands that they end their oppression and
share with the poor. God longs for the salvation of the rich as much
as the salvation of the poor. God desires fulfillment and joy for all
his creatures. But that in no way contradicts the fact that God is on
the side of the poor. Genuine biblical repentance and conversion
lead people to turn from all sin—including economic oppression.[6]
Salvation for the rich will include liberation from their involvement
in injustice. Thus God's desire for the salvation and fulfillment of
the rich is in complete harmony with his special concern for the
poor. The God revealed in Scripture is on the side of the poor and
oppressed.

God's concern for the poor seems astonishing and boundless.
At the pivotal points of revelation history, Yahweh was at work
liberating the oppressed. We can only begin to fathom the depth of
his identification with the poor disclosed in the incarnation. His
passion for justice compels him to obliterate rich persons and
societies that oppress the poor and neglect the needy. Consequently, God's people—if they are indeed his people—follow in
the footsteps of the God of the poor.

II
"THAT THERE MAY BE EQUALITY":
ECONOMIC RELATIONSHIPS AMONG THE PEOPLE OF GOD

The New Community of Jesus' Disciples. Jesus walked the
roads and footpaths of Galilee announcing the startling news that
the long expected kingdom of peace and righteousness was at
hand. Economic relationships in the new community of his followers were a powerful sign confirming this awesome announcement.

The Hebrew prophets had inspired the hope of a future messianic kingdom of peace, righteousness and justice. The essence of
the good news which Jesus proclaimed was that the expected

messianic kingdom had come. Certainly the kingdom that Jesus announced disappointed popular Jewish expectations. He did not recruit an army to drive out the Romans. He did not attempt to establish a free Jewish state. But neither did he remain alone as an isolated, individualistic prophet. He called and trained disciples. He established a visible community of disciples joined together by their unconditional submission to him as Lord. His new community began to live the values of the promised kingdom which was already breaking into the present. As a result, all relationships, even economic ones, were transformed in the community of Jesus' followers.

Jesus and his disciples shared a common purse (Jn. 12:6 and 13:29). Judas administered the common fund, buying provisions or giving to the poor at Jesus' direction (Jn. 13:29). Nor did this new community of sharing end with Jesus and the Twelve. It included a number of women whom Jesus had healed. The women traveled with Jesus and the disciples, sharing their financial resources with them (Lk. 8:1-3).

From this perspective, some of Jesus' words gain new meaning and power. Consider Jesus' advice to the rich young man in this context.

> When Jesus asked the rich young man to sell his goods and give to the poor, he did not say, "Become destitute and friendless." Rather, he said, "Come, follow me" (Mt. 19:21). In other words, he invited him to join a community of sharing and love, where his security would not be based on individual property holdings, but on openness to the Spirit and on the loving care of new-found brothers and sisters.[7]

Jesus invited the rich young man to share the joyful common life of his new kingdom.

Jesus' words in Mark 10:29-30 have long puzzled me: "Truly, I say to you, there is no one who has left houses or brothers or sisters or mother or father or children or lands, for my sake and the Gospel, who will not receive a hundredfold *now in this time, houses and brothers and sisters and mothers and children and lands,* with persecutions, and in the age to come eternal life."

Matthew 6 contains a similar saying. We are all very—indeed, embarrassingly—familiar with the way Jesus urged his followers to enjoy a carefree life unburdened by anxiety over food, clothing and possessions (vv. 25-33). But he ended his advice with a promise too good to be true: "But seek first his kingdom and his righteousness and all these things (i.e., food, clothing, etc.) shall be yours as well" (v. 33).

Jesus' promise used to seem at least a trifle naive. But his words suddenly came alive with fantastic meaning when I read them in the context of the new community of Jesus' followers. Jesus began a new social order, a new kingdom of faithful followers who were to be completely available to each other.

The common purse of Jesus' disciples symbolized that unlimited liability for each other. In that kind of new community, there would truly be genuine economic security. One would indeed receive one hundred times more loving brothers and sisters than before. The economic resources available in difficult times would in fact be compounded a hundredfold and more. All the resources of the entire community of obedient disciples would be available to anyone in need. To be sure, that kind of unselfish, sharing life-style would challenge surrounding society so pointedly that there would be persecutions. But even in the most desperate days, the promise would not be empty. Even if persecution led to death, children of martyred parents would receive new mothers and fathers in the community of believers. In the community of the redeemed, all relationships are being transformed. The common purse shared by Jesus and his first followers vividly demonstrates that Jesus repeated and deepened the old covenant's call for transformed economic relationships among the people of God.

The Jerusalem Church. However embarrassing it may be to some, the massive economic sharing of the earliest Christian Church is indisputable. "Now the company of those who believed were of one heart and soul, and no one said that any of the things which he possessed was his own, but they had everything in common" (Acts 4:32). Everywhere in the early chapters of Acts, the evidence is abundant and unambiguous (Acts 2:43-7; 4:32-7; 5:1-11; 6:1-7). The early Church continued the pattern of economic sharing practiced by Jesus.

Economic sharing in the Jerusalem church started in the earliest period. Immediately after reporting the 3,000 conversions at Pentecost, Acts notes that "all who believed were together and had all things in common" (2:44). Whenever anyone was in need, they shared. Giving surplus income to needy brothers and sisters was not enough. They regularly dipped into capital reserves, selling property to aid the needy. Barnabas sold a field he owned (4:36-37). Ananias and Sapphira sold property, although they lied about the price. God's promise to Israel (Deut. 15:4) that faithful obedience would eliminate poverty among his people came true! *"There was not a needy person among them,* for as many as were possessors of lands or houses sold them . . . and distribution was made to each as any had need" (4:34-35).

Two millennia later, the texts still throb with the first community's joy and excitement. They ate meals together "with glad and generous heart" (2:46). They experienced an exciting unity as all sensed they "were of one heart and soul" (4:32). They were not isolated individuals struggling alone to follow Jesus. A new community transforming all areas of life became a joyful reality. The new converts at Pentecost "devoted themselves to the apostles' teaching and fellowship, to the breaking of bread and the prayers" (2:42). The earliest Jerusalem Christians experienced such joyful oneness in Christ that they promptly engaged in sweeping economic sharing.

What was the precise nature of the Jerusalem church's costly *koinonia?* The earliest Church did not insist on absolute economic equality, nor did it abolish private property. Sharing was voluntary, not compulsory. But love for brothers and sisters was so overwhelming that many freely abandoned legal claims to private possessions. "No one said that any of the things that he possessed was his own" (4:32). That does not mean that everyone donated everything. Later in Acts, we see that John Mark's mother Mary still owned her house (12:12). Others also undoubtedly retained some private property.

The tense of the Greek verbs in Acts 2:45 and 4:34 confirms this interpretation. The verbs are in the imperfect tense. In Greek, the imperfect tense denotes continued, repeated action over an extended period of time. Thus the meaning is: "They often sold possessions." Or: "They were in the habit of regularly bringing the proceeds of what was being sold." The text does not suggest that the community decided to abolish all private property and everyone instantly sold everything. Rather it suggests that over a period of time, whenever there was need, believers regularly sold lands and houses to aid the needy.

What then was the essence of the transformed economic relationships in the Jerusalem church? I think the best way to describe their practice is to speak of unlimited liability and total availability. Their sharing was not superficial or occasional. Regularly and repeatedly, they sold possessions and goods and distributed them to all, *"as any had need."* If the need was greater than current cash reserves, they sold property. They simply gave until the needs were met. The needs of the sister and brother, not legal property rights or future financial security, were decisive. The brothers and sisters made their financial resources unconditionally available to each other. Oneness in Christ for the earliest Christian community meant unlimited economic liability for the total economic availability to the other members of the people of God.

The costly sharing of the first Church stands as a constant challenge to Christians of all ages. They dared to give concrete, visible expression to the oneness of believers. In the new messianic community of Jesus' first followers after Pentecost, God was redeeming all relationships.

Whatever the beauty and appeal, of such an example, however, was it not a vision which quickly faded? Most people believe that. But the actual practice of the early Church proves exactly the contrary.

The Pauline Collection. Paul broadened the vision of economic sharing among the people of God in a dramatic way. He devoted a great deal of time to raising money for Jewish Christians among Gentile congregations. In the process, he broadened *intra*-church assistance within one local church into *inter*-church sharing among all the scattered congregations of believers. From the time of the exodus, God had taught his chosen people to exhibit transformed economic relations among themselves. With Peter and Paul, however, biblical religion moved beyond one ethnic group and became a universal, multi-ethnic faith. Paul's collection demonstrates that the oneness of that new, multi-ethnic body of believers entails dramatic economic sharing across ethnic and geographic lines.

For several years, Paul devoted much time and energy to his great collection for the Jerusalem church. He discussed his concern in several letters (Col. 2:10; Rom. 15:22-28; 1 Cor. 16:1-4; 2 Cor. 7—9). Paul arranged for the collection in the churches of Macedonia, Galatia, Asia, Corinth, Ephesus and probably elsewhere.

Paul knew he faced certain danger and possible death, but he still insisted on personally accompanying the offering for the Jerusalem church. It was while delivering this financial assistance that Paul was arrested for the last time (Acts 24:17). His letter to the Romans shows that he was not blind to the danger (Rom. 15:31). Repeatedly, friends and prophets warned Paul as he and the representatives of the contributing churches journeyed toward Jerusalem (Acts 21:4, 10-14). But Paul had a deep conviction that this financial symbol of Christian unity mattered far more than even his own life. "What are you doing, weeping and breaking my heart?" he chided friends imploring him not to accompany the others to Jerusalem. "For I am ready not only to be imprisoned but even to die at Jerusalem for the name of the Lord Jesus" (Acts 21:13). And he continued the journey. His passionate commitment to economic sharing with brothers and sisters led to his final arrest and martyrdom.

Why was Paul so concerned with the financial problems of the Jerusalem church? Because of his understanding of Christian fellowship *(koinonia)*. *Koinonia* is an extremely important concept in Paul's theology. And it is central in his discussion of the collection.

The word *koinonia* means fellowship with, or participation in, something or someone. Believers enjoy fellowship with the Lord Jesus (1 Cor. 1:9). Experiencing the *koinonia* of Jesus means having his righteousness imputed to us. It also entails sharing in the self-sacrificing, cross-bearing life he lived (Phil. 3:8-10). Nowhere is the Christian's fellowship with Christ experienced more powerfully than in the Eucharist. Sharing in the Eucharist draws the believer into a participation *(koinonia)* in the mystery of the cross.

The cup of blessing which we bless, is it not a participation *(koinonia)* in the blood of Christ? The bread which we break, is it not a participation (*koinonia*) in the body of Christ? (1 Cor. 10:16)

Paul's immediate inference—in the very next verse—is that *koinonia* with Christ inevitably involves *koinonia* with all the members of the body of Christ. "Because there is one bread, we who are many are one body, for we all partake of the one bread" (v. 17). As he taught in Ephesians 2, Christ's death for Jew and Gentile, male and female, has broken down all ethnic, sexual, and cultural dividing walls. In Christ, there is one new person, one new body of believers. When the brothers and sisters share the one bread and the common cup in the Lord's supper, they symbolize and actualize their participation in the one body of Christ.

That is why the class divisions at Corinth so horrified Paul. Wealthy Christians, apparently, were feasting at the eucharistic celebration while poor believers went hungry. Paul angrily denied that they were eating the Lord's supper at all (1 Cor 11:20-22). In fact they were profaning the Lord's body and blood because they did not discern his body (vv. 27-29). What did Paul mean by not discerning the Lord's body? He meant that they failed to realize that their membership in the one body of Christ was infinitely more important than the class or ethnic differences which divided them. One drinks judgment on oneself if one does not perceive that eucharistic fellowship with Christ is totally incompatible with living a practical denial of the unity and fellowship of all believers in the body of Christ. As long as one Christian anywhere in the world is hungry, the eucharistic celebration of all Christians everywhere is incomplete.

For Paul, this intimate fellowship in the body of Christ had concrete economic implications. Paul used precisely this same word, *koinonia,* to designate financial sharing among believers. Sometimes he employed the word *koinonia* as a virtual synonym for "collection." He spoke of the "liberality of the fellowship" (*koinonia*) that the Corinthians' generous offering would demonstrate (2 Cor. 9:13). He employed the same language to report the Macedonian Christians' offering for Jerusalem. It seemed good to the Macedonians, he said, "to make fellowship (*koinonia*) with the poor among the saints at Jerusalem" (Rom. 15:26). Indeed, this financial sharing was just one part of a total fellowship. The Gentile

Christians had come to share in (he uses the verb form of *koinonia*) the spiritual blessings of the Jews. Therefore it was fitting for the Gentiles to share their material resources. Economic sharing was an obvious and crucial part of Christian fellowship for St. Paul.

Paul's guideline for sharing in the body of believers is startling. The norm he suggested is something like economic equality among the people of God. "I do not mean that others should be eased and you burdened, but that as a matter of equality your abundance at the present time should supply their want, so that their abundance may supply your want, that there may be equality" (2 Cor. 8:13-14). To support his principle, Paul quoted from the biblical story of manna. "As it is written, he who gathered much had nothing over, and he who gathered little had no lack" (v. 15).

According to the Exodus account, when God started sending daily manna to the Israelites in the wilderness, Moses commanded the people to gather only as much as they needed for one day (Ex. 16:13-21). One *omer* (about four pints) per person would be enough, Moses said. Some greedy souls, however, apparently tried to gather more than they could use. But when they measured what they had gathered, they discovered that they all had just one *omer* per person. The account concludes: "He that gathered much had nothing over and he that gathered little had no lack" (Ex. 16:18).

Paul quoted from the biblical account of the manna to support his guideline for economic sharing. Just as God had insisted on equal portions of manna for all his people in the wilderness, so now the Corinthians should give "that there may be equality" in the body of Christ.

It may seem startling and disturbing to rich Christians in the northern hemisphere, but the biblical text clearly shows that Paul enunciated the principle of economic equality among the people of God to guide the Corinthians in their giving. *"It is a question of equality*. At the moment your surplus meets their need, but one day your need may be met from their surplus. *The aim is equality"* (New English Bible).

However interesting it may be, what relevance does the economic sharing at Jerusalem and Corinth have for the contemporary Church?

Certainly the Church today need not slavishly imitate every

detail of the life of the early Church depicted in Acts. But that does not mean that we can simply dismiss the economic sharing described in Acts and the Pauline letters.

Over and over again God specifically commanded his people to live together in community in such a way that they would avoid extremes of wealth and poverty. That is the point of the Old Testament legislation on the jubilee and the sabbatical year. That is the point of the legislation on tithing, gleaning and loans.[8] Jesus, our only perfect model, shared a common purse with the new community of his disciples. The first Church in Jerusalem and St. Paul in his collection were implementing what the Old Testament and Jesus commanded.

The powerful evangelistic impact of the economic sharing at Jerusalem indicates that God approved and blessed the practice of the Jerusalem church. When Scripture commands transformed economic relationships among God's people in some places and describes God's blessing on his people as they implement these commands in other places, then we can be sure that we have discovered a normative pattern for the Church today.

What is striking in fact is the fundamental continuity of biblical teaching and practice at this point. The Bible repeatedly and pointedly reveals that God wills transformed economic relationships among his people. Paul's collection was simply an application of the basic principle of the jubilee. The mechanism, of course, was different because the people of God were now a multi-ethnic body living in different lands. But the principle was the same. Since the Greeks at Corinth were now part of the people of God, they were to share with the poor Jewish Christians at Jerusalem—that there might be equality!

Conclusion

By way of conclusion, I want to sketch a few implications of these biblical themes for contemporary Christian concern for world hunger.

A. In the Church. Central to any Christian strategy on world hunger must be a radical call for the Church to be the Church. One of the most glaring weaknesses of the churches' social action in the past few decades is that the Church concentrated too exclusively on political solutions. In effect, Church leaders tried to persuade government to legislate what they could not persuade their Church members to live. And politicians quickly sensed that the daring declarations and frequent Washington delegations represented generals without troops. Only if the body of Christ is already beginning to live a radically new model of economic sharing will our demand for political change have integrity and impact.

Tragically we must confess that present economic relationships in the worldwide body of Christ are unbiblical and sinful; indeed they are a desecration of the body and blood of our Lord. It is a sinful abomination for a small fraction of the world's Christians living in the northern hemisphere to grow richer year by year while our brothers and sisters in the third world ache and suffer for lack of minimal health care, minimal education, and even just enough food to escape starvation.

We are like the rich Corinthian Christians who feasted without sharing their food with the poor members of the Church (1 Cor. 11:20-29). Like them we fail today to discern the reality of the one worldwide body of Christ. The tragic consequence is that we profane the body and blood of the Lord Jesus we worship. U.S. Christians spent 5.7 billion dollars on new church construction alone in the six years from 1967-1972. Would we go on building lavishly furnished expensive church plants if members of our own congregations were starving? Do we not flatly contradict St. Paul if we live as if African or Latin American members of the body of Christ are less a part of us than the members of our home congregations?

A radical call to repentance so that the Church becomes the Church must be central to a viable contemporary Christian strategy for reducing world hunger and restructuring international economic relationships. Unless the Church begins to live a new model of economic sharing in the local congregations in each geographic area, and in the one worldwide body of Christ, any political appeal for governmental action will be a tragic, irrelevant farce.

The Church is the most universal body in the world today. It has the opportunity to live a new corporate model of economic sharing at a desperate moment in world history. If even one-quarter of the Christians in the northern hemisphere had the courage to live the biblical vision of economic equality in the worldwide body of Christ, the governments of our dangerously divided global village might also be persuaded to legislate the sweeping changes needed to avoid disaster.

B. In Secular Society. The centrality of the Church as the new community for Christian social concern by no means entails the view that working to restructure secular political and economic systems is inappropriate or irrelevant.

From the preceding analysis, we can summarize a few of the fundamental biblical principles and norms we need to keep in mind as we think of structural change in society. The most basic theological presupposition is that the sovereign Lord of this universe is always at work liberating the poor and oppressed and destroying the rich and mighty because of their injustice.

Second, extremes of wealth and poverty are displeasing to the God of the Bible. Third, Yahweh wills institutionalized structures (rather than mere charity) which systematically and regularly reduce the gap between the rich and the poor.[9] Fourth, although they do not suggest a wooden, legalistic egalitarianism, the biblical patterns for economic sharing (e.g., the Jubilee, the Pauline collection) all push toward a closer approximation of economic equality. Fifth, persons are vastly more valuable than property. Private property is legitimate, but since God is the only absolute owner, our right to acquire and use property is definitely limited. The human right to the resources necessary to earn a just living overrides any notion of absolute private ownership.[10]

The last principle is particularly significant for us. Some countries like the United States and the USSR have a bountiful supply of natural resources within their national boundaries. But it by no means follows that they have an absolute right to use these resources as they please solely for the advantage of their own citizens. If we believe God's word, then we must conclude that the human right of all persons to earn a just living clearly supersedes the United States' right to use its natural resources for itself. We are only stewards, not absolute owners. The absolute owner is the God of the poor and he insists that the earth's resources be shared.

NOTES

1. This essay is taken from sections of my *Rich Christians in an Age of Hunger: A Biblical Study* (Downers Grove: Inter Varsity Press, 1977), chapters 3-4. For the pertinent bibliography, see the notes to those chapters.

2. For a discussion of the relationship of evangelism and social action, see my "Evangelism, Salvation and Social Justice: Definitions and Interrelationships," *International Review of Mission,* July, 1975, pp. 251-267.

3. Cf. also 1 Sam. 2:2-8; Lk. 6:20-25.

4. Cf. also Jer. 22; Ps. 10; Is. 3:13-25.

5. Cf. also Is. 59:3ff; Am. 5:21ff.

6. For a discussion of sin as both "personal" and "social," see *Rich Christians in an Age of Hunger,* chap. 6.

7. Richard K. Taylor, *Economics and the Gospel* Philadelphia: United Church Press, 1973), p. 21.

8. For a discussion of these items, see *Rich Christians in an Age of Hunger,* pp. 88-95.

9. *Ibid.*

10. *Ibid.,* pp. 113-117.

Biblical Sources of Stewardship

Willard M. Swartley

The word "stewardship" as it is used and misused today is not a biblical term. In the Bible, individuals are stewards in someone's household (Gen. 43:19; 44:4; 1 Kings 15:18) and Christian believers are called to be stewards of God's mysteries *(oikonomoi),* meaning "Gospel" or "the economy which includes Gentiles for salvation" (1 Cor. 4:1; Gal. 4:2; Eph. 1:10; 3:2; 1 Pet. 4:10).[1] Only in two parables is the term steward *(oikonomos)* used in the sense of "stewardship of possessions" (Lk. 12:42; 16:1-4), but even there when the Christian application of the parable is made, the term changes to "servant" *(doulos*—Lk 12:43; cf. also Mt. 25:21). Nevertheless, there is a concept of stewardship that is everywhere present in biblical thought, a concept or view that regards mankind responsible before God for the use of the created world, the social health of the people, and the maximal development of each person's abilities for the upbuilding of the community.

Of the many ways that one might develop the biblical teachings on stewardship, this study is based on theological affirmations for its main outline and then develops certain themes as sub-topics as follows: (1) God the Creator: Creation and Stewardship; (2) God the Redeemer: Covenant and Stewardship; and (3) God of Jesus Christ: The Christian Meaning of Stewardship.

I
GOD THE CREATOR: CREATION AND STEWARDSHIP

Because God created the world and all that is in it he is the owner of everything. "The earth is the Lord's and the fullness thereof, the world and those who dwell therein" (Ps. 24:1). "For every beast of the forest is mine, the cattle on a thousand hills" (Ps. 50:10). God asked Job, "Who has given to me that I should repay him? Whatever is under the whole heaven is mine" (Jb. 41:11)

The account of the creation also makes it clear . . . that God is the real owner of all material things as well as of spiritual reality, and these things have been given by God to men as stewards. "Blessed art thou, O Lord. . . . Both riches and honor come from thee. . . . But who am I . . . that we should be able thus to offer willingly? For all things come from thee, and of thy own have we given thee" (1 Chr. 29:10-14).[2]

The biblical perspective affirms that stewardship is not stewardship of one's own possessions, but stewardship of *what belongs to God*. Stewardship is not a way of managing of *our* possessions; it means rather that we care for what *God* has entrusted *to* us.

Mankind as Created

This understanding of stewardship is rooted in the biblical view that mankind was created in God's image *(tselem)*. Biblical scholars have pointed out a significant relationship between mankind's creation in God's image and mankind's responsibilty to "have dominion" over all creation (Gen. 1:26-30). Gerhard von Rad, e.g., comments on this relationship in his esteemed commentary on Genesis:

This commission to rule is not considered as belonging to the definition of God's image, but it is its consequence, i.e., that for which man is capable because of it. . . . Just as powerful earthly kings, to indicate their claim to dominion, erect an image of themselves in the provinces of their empire where they do not personally appear, so man is placed upon earth in God's image as God's sovereign emblem. He is really only God's representative, summoned to maintain and enforce God's claim to dominion over the earth.[3]

Precisely in this relationship between "being in God's image" and "having dominion over the creation" do we grasp hold of a biblical understanding which may be here designated by the term "stewardship." Biblical synonyms for this concept are (covenant) "faithfulness," "knowledge of God," "obedience," "justice," "righteousness," and "love for God and one's neighbor." The burden of the Bible concerns the behavior of humankind. Further, the criteria for mankind's accountability before God are, on the one hand, the potential to be God's image, thus extending God's presence in the world, and, on the other hand, the command to take delegated responsibility for *God's* creation.

In relation to creation and use of the world's resources, we are expected to care for them as God cares for them. In relation to our fellow humanity, the challenge to be God's image means that we treat them both as God treats them and as we would treat God. From this context we understand Jesus' own appeal: "Inasmuch as you did it (not) unto one of the least of these, you did it (not) to me" (Mt. 25:40, 45).

The biblical theology of the primeval period (Gen. 1-11) portrays the interrelationship of the representative man's—thus all mankind's—origin, welfare, and destiny with that of both creation's and fellow humanity's origin, welfare, and destiny. The first creation account makes this point by locating mankind's creation on the sixth day together with all the other land animals. Further, in the liturgical structure, day six is a matching parallel to day three on which the earth and vegetation were created, thus showing the biblical view of man's relatedness to the earth and all its life. The second creation account emphasizes the same point by stressing that man, *adam,* was created from the ground, *adamah.* Adam is made from the *adamah* (2:7). When *man* (adam) sinned, the *ground* (adamah) was cursed (3:16) and man's own curse included his struggle against the thorns and thistles of the *ground* and eventual "return to the *ground,* for out of it" mankind was made (3:19). When Cain kills his brother Abel, Cain's offering from the fruit of the *ground* offends his Creator because his brother's blood is crying from the *ground.* Therefore, Cain is "cursed from the *ground"* and "the *ground* . . . shall no longer yield to (him) its strength."

Upon the birth of Noah, a new hope from and for the *ground* emerges: "Out of the *ground* which the Lord has cursed, this one shall bring us relief from our work and from the toil of our hands"(5:29). The judgment of the flood, blotting out fallen mankind, is a purification of the "face of the *ground*" (6:7) and God's rainbow promise is to "never again curse the *ground* because of man" (8:21).

This biblical theology of creation clearly teaches an intrinsic relationship between humankind and the earth, a relationship which hinges upon human morality. The theology of Genesis 3—4 clearly teaches that mankind's primal sin is refusal to *be* God's *image*. Instead of representing God's rule and ownership, mankind chooses "to be like God" (3:5), usurping God's rights for themselves. Precisely in that choice to rebel against God, both mankind *(adam)* and the ground *(adamah)* experience the curse of the Creator. Because mankind was created both from the earth and for dominion over the earth, the fruit or thistles of the ground shape humankind's ecstasy or agony.

Morality and the Ecosystem

The Old Testament prophets preached this creation-theology to the apostate nation of Israel. One such sermon comes from the prophet Hosea:

Hear the word of the Lord, O people of Israel;
for the Lord has a controversy with the inhabitants of the land.
There is no faithfulness or kindness, and no knowledge of God
  in the land;
there is swearing, lying, killing, stealing, and committing adultery;
they break all bounds and murder follows murder.
Therefore the land mourns, and all who dwell in it languish,
and also the beasts of the field, and the birds of the air;
and even the fish of the sea are taken away (4:1-3).

Scholars classify this particular paragraph in Hosea as a *rib-*

oracle, because the Hebrew word translated as "controversy" is *rib*. The word *rib* is a legal term and might well be translated "lawsuit." God is suing the people of the covenant for breaking the terms of the covenant. The thought-sequence of the text is as follows: The Lord of the covenant sues the people because their corporate life is pagan, and therefore "the land mourns," or vice versa, the barrenness of the land results from the people's immorality which is cause for covenant lawsuit. This is the prophetic logic which makes ecological welfare dependent upon the people's moral and spiritual condition. The same type of sermon recurs frequently in the prophets, e.g., Isaiah 24:4-5, Jeremiah 4:18-28, and Micah 6:1-15.

The text in Micah merits attention. Like Hosea 4, Micah 6 is another *rib*-oracle, a covenant lawsuit against the people. In verses 1-2 the mountains are the enduring foundations of the earth which "hear the case" and function as a jury. Verses 3-5 recite Yahweh's beneficent acts for the people. Verses 6-7 register Yahweh's complaint against Israel's attempt to substitute sacrifice for justice, followed by the classic prophetic statement of the morality Yahweh requires (v. 8). Then in verses 9-12 Yahweh cries out accusations against the people. The people have no defense. Hence God issues the sentence:

Therefore I have begun to smite you,
making you desolate because of your sins.
You shall eat, but not be satisfied,
and there shall be hunger in your inward parts;
you shall put away, but not save,
and what you save I will give to the sword.
You shall sow, but not reap;
you shall tread olives, but not anoint yourselves with oil;
you shall tread grapes, but not drink wine (6:13-15).

On the basis of these several insights into the pattern of biblical thought, it is clear that the issues of hunger and ecology are moral issues. The life of humankind is inextricably related to the ground, in its origin, welfare, and destiny. God's call in creation is to the stewardship of the *divine* dominion over the earth. But mankind's fallenness regularly manifests itself in independent dominion and curses upon the ground (Gen. 3).[4] It is therefore imperative to look toward the ethics of redemption to discover the shape of the life liberated from the bondage of the fall's curse.

II
GOD THE REDEEMER: COVENANT AND STEWARDSHIP

If one is to correctly grasp the significance of Old Testament teachings on stewardship, it is imperative to see these teachings within the context of the covenant. As noted above in the lawsuit oracles, Israel's ethical accountability was determined by the covenant relationship. Recent Old Testament studies have shown that Israel's covenant form, similar to and dependent upon the form of the Hittite suzerainty treaties of the fourteenth century B.C., regards legal and ethical prescriptions as expected response within the covenant relationship established by Yahweh with the people.[5] From this perspective, the following discussion surveys Old Testament teachings on stewardship of the land, covenant justice, and norms for judgment.

Stewardship of the Land

God owns the land: that was the fundamental conviction of the Old Testament. The Holiness Code of Leviticus (19:26) puts it this way:

> The land shall not be sold in perpetuity, for the land is mine; for you are strangers and sojourners with me. And in all the country you shall possess, you shall grant a redemption of the land (25:23-24).

This divine claim upon the land was the basis for the sabbatical year when the land lay fallow and the fiftieth year when each family clan received anew its original land allotment (Lev. 25:1-12). The basis for such radical social legislation was (1) theological: the land is a *gift* from Yahweh (25:2); (2) humanitarian: "You shall not wrong one another" (25:14, 17); and (3) rooted in redemptive covenant history: "For I am the Lord your God . . . who brought you out of the land of Egypt to give you the land of Canaan, and to be your God" (25:17, 37). The warfare of the conquest submitted to the same theological conviction: God fought *for* his people and they received the land as a gift (Ex. 14:14; 23:20-33; Jos. 5:13-15; 24:12-13).

From this theological perspective central to Israel's self-identity, one understands the prophets' indignation over land-grabbing:

> Woe to those who . . . covet fields, and seize them;
> and houses, and take them away;
> They oppress a man and his house,
> a man and his inheritance (Mi. 2:1-2)

> Woe to those who join house to house,
> who add field to field . . . (Is. 5:8a).

One also understands Elijah's and Yahweh's blazing anger against Ahab and Jezebel for plotting the acquisition of Naboth's vineyard (1 Kgs. 21:1-26), Jeremiah's plea to institute jubilee and thus avert exile (Jer. 34), and the proverbial injunction: "Remove not the ancient landmark . . ." (Prv. 22:28; 23:10; Jb. 24:2; Deut. 19:14; 27:17).

This teaching regarding God's ownership of the land clearly teaches the point earlier noted: stewardship is not stewardship of one's own possession but stewardship of *what belongs to God.* Stewardship is not a way of managing *our* possessions; it rather affirms that we are stewards of what *God* entrusts *to* us. And because God remains owner, our neighbor's welfare can never be slighted, for God is Father of us both (Mal. 2:10).

Covenant Justice

Any effort to understand biblical perspectives on stewardship must squarely face the prophets' passionate pronouncements on justice. Abraham Heschel says it well:

Instead of dealing with the timeless issues of being and becoming, of matter and form, of definitions and demonstrations, [the reader of the prophets] is thrown into orations about widows and orphans, about the corruption of judges and affairs of the market place. Instead of showing us a way through the elegant mansions of the mind, the prophets take us to the slums. The world is a proud place, full of beauty, but the prophets are scandalized, and rave as if the whole world were a slum. . . . To us a single act of injustice—cheating in business, exploitation of the poor—is slight; to the prophets, a disaster. To us injustice is injurious to the welfare of the people; to the prophets it is a deathblow to existence; to us, an episode; to them, a catastrophe, a threat to the world.[6]

The prophets spoke for God and understood God in accord with the testimony of the psalmist:

Righteousness and justice are the foundation of thy throne; steadfast love and faithfulness go before thee (Ps. 89:14).

In its basic form the entire system of sabbath, sabbatical, and jubilee were expressions of God's justice. The humanitarian purpose of the sabbath enabled the servants to rest as well as the masters (Deut. 5:12-14). The sabbatical provisions gave servants freedom to choose anew their masters (Ex. 21:1-6) and canceled debts in order to ensure economic equality (Deut. 15:1-6). The most fundamental guarantee of justice was the jubilean redistribution of property. In addition to these specific provisions, the social legislation for Israel's life repeatedly protected the rights of the poor and the community's responsibility for the poor, the widow, orphan, and stranger (Ex. 22:21-24; 23:9-11; Lev. 19:9-10; 25:25-28, 35-55; Deut. 15:4-11; 23:25-26; 24:19-22). There was also the *second* tithe, to be paid every three years, for the dispossessed Levite, the fatherless, the widow, and the sojourner (Deut. 14:29; 26:13). Further, these responsibilities were all rooted in Israel's covenant relationship to God (Lev. 25:17, 38; Ex. 23:9b, 13).

As Philip F. Mulhern points out in his excellent study of dedicated poverty,[7] the poor were regarded as specially devout

before Yahweh (e.g., Ps. 34; Is. 21:6, etc.) so that by the time of the
Qumran community the community of the poor *(anawim)* were
identified with "the elect" and the coming messianic community.[8]

The prophetic passion for justice is therefore part and parcel
of God's concern for the poor. As José Miranda points out in his
disturbing book entitled *Marx and the Bible,* the Old Testament
terms for justice *(mishpat)* and righteousness *(zedaqah)* are virtually synonymous. In addition to appearing together in synonymous
parallelisms thirty-four times, the two roots *(spht* and *sdk)* are
paired together in thirty-two other instances.[9]

In the "golden text" of the prophetic ethic, Amos declares:

> Let justice roll down like waters,
> and righteousness like an everflowing stream (5:24)

Micah's classical summary is similar:

> He has showed you, O man, what is good;
> and what does the Lord require of you
> but to do justice, and to love kindness,
> and to walk humbly with your God (6:8)?

Isaiah also, in his lament and word-pun over Israel's perversion of
values, enunciates the same divine standard:

> God looked for justice *(mishpat),*
> but behold, bloodshed *(mishpah);*
> for righteousness *(zedaqah),*
> but behold, a cry *(ze'aqah).* (5:7b)

How readily Isaiah's lament is applied to the 1960's and 1970's
of our day! In the 1960's God looked for justice *(mishpat),* but,
behold, only bloodshed *(mishpah).* In the 1970's he is looking for
righteousness *(zedaqah),* but, behold, only the *cries* of the poor
and hungry *(ze'aqah).* In the same integral way that justice and
righteousness are the foundations of God's throne (Ps. 89:14), so in
the same way justice is foundational to stewardship.

Milo Kauffman, in his book on Christian stewardship, applies
the prophetic ethic to stewardship as follows:

The prophet Amos cried out against Israel because they "sold the righteous for silver, and the poor for a pair of shoes" (2:6). He charges, in chapter three, that their beautiful houses are full of loot from thefts and banditry. Micah charges Israel with driving widows from their homes and stripping children of every God-given right (2:2). One cannot love God, be a true steward of God, and treat his fellow men thus. He will realize that his attitude toward people reflects his attitude toward God.[10]

Norms for Judgment

While the prophetic literature of the Old Testament is brim-full with calls to justice which in turn function as norms for judgment, three texts are particularly noteworthy in this regard—one pre-exilic, one exilic, and one post-exilic.

The first is Jeremiah's temple court sermon. Jeremiah condemned the people for trusting in the security of the temple. For Jeremiah, the only alternative to imminent doom was pursuit of justice:

For if you truly amend your ways and your doings, if you truly execute justice one with another, if you do not oppress the alien, the fatherless or the widow, or shed innocent blood in this place, and if you do not go after other gods to your own hurt, then I will let you dwell in this place, in the land that I gave of old to your fathers for ever (7:5-7).

Later on during the exile when charging the downhearted exiles to responsibility for their own destiny, Ezekiel defined three times the righteousness that God demanded from his people as consisting of not oppressing anyone, restoring to the debtor his pledge, committing no robbery, giving bread to the hungry, and covering the naked (7:7-18).

In another prophetic text addressed to the post-exilic community, Isaiah contrasted the rituals of fasting to the fast of ethical sensitivity (58:12). The fast which God demands is the fast that frees the oppressed, breaks every yoke, shares bread with the hungry, houses the homeless poor, and covers the naked (58:6-7, 10).

The text in Jeremiah was addressed to the nation, Ezekiel's to the individual, and Isaiah's to the people as a corporate group. In each case the norms of judgment are the same. Before exile, during exile, and after exile, God's standard stands as the criterion by which the people are saved or doomed. Nor do the norms for the judgment of the Christian change in the New Testament, as will be shown below. The call to stewardship is a call to practice the justice of God.

III
GOD OF JESUS CHRIST:
THE CHRISTIAN MEANING OF STEWARDSHIP

Jesus Fulfills the Sabbath and Jubilee

Each of the four Gospels records conflict between Jesus and the Jewish leaders over Jesus' sabbath practices. The critical issue in all instances consisted of Jesus' insistence that deeds of helpfulness, and, specifically, the restoration of the sick to health, do not violate sabbath intentions, but rather fulfill the true meaning of the sabbath (Mk. 2:28—3:6; par. in Mt. and Lk.; Jn. 5 and 9). Not only does Jesus do what the humanitarian purpose of the sabbath stood for (Deut. 5:12-14), but he also pronounces himself "lord of the sabbath," declaring that the "sabbath was made for man, and not man for the sabbath" (Mk. 2:27-28).

Luke's two-volume work, the Gospel and Acts, appears to emphasize that Jesus fulfills the justice of the jubilee year. Jesus' inauguration speech in the Nazareth synagogue, quoting Isaiah 61:1-2a, focuses on the social righteousness of the jubilee year, "the acceptable year of the Lord":

"The Spirit of the Lord is upon me,
because he has anointed me to preach good news to the poor.
He has sent me to proclaim release to the captives

and recovering of sight to the blind,
to set at liberty those who are oppressed,
to proclaim the acceptable year of the Lord." . . .
And he began to say to them,
"Today this Scripture has been fulfilled in your hearing"
  (4:18-19, 21).

As John Howard Yoder points out in his stimulating study, *The Politics of Jesus,* numerous emphases in Luke's Gospel, found also in Mark and Matthew, coincide with the jubilean emphases, most notably Mary's Magnificat, in which the lowly are exalted and the hungry fed (1:52-53), the call to kingly servanthood at Jesus' baptism (3:22), Jesus' resistance of the temptations to kingship on worldly socio-political terms (4:1-14), Jesus' call to suffering discipleship (12:49—14:36; 22:25ff.), and the Lord's Prayer itself (11:3-4), which uses a word for "forgiveness" of sins and debts regularly used in the debt-cancellation contract of jubilee.[11]

The widely recognized Lukan emphasis on blessings for the poor and woes upon the rich (6:20, 24) supports a jubilean understanding of Jesus (see also chs. 12, 16, the end of 18 and the beginning of 19).[12] In Acts Jesus' followers practiced community of goods so that there "was not a needy person among them" (4:32-34; 2:43-46), widows' material needs were met (6:1-6), and the church at Antioch sent a relief gift to the poor in Jerusalem (11:27-30; Gal. 2:10). Jesus and the early Church thus continued the same kind of concern for the poor and needy as was expressed in the Torah and the prophets.

Luke's Gospel stresses other points that also fit well with a Christian vision of the jubilean justice: the prominent role of women: Elizabeth, Mary, Anna, the women from Galilee among Jesus' disciples (8:1-3), Martha and Mary, and the women at the tomb; Jesus' acceptance of the outsiders and outcasts so that the forgiven prostitute and prodigal have a future in Jesus' messianic community (7:36-50; 15); and the clear welcome of Samaritans and Gentiles into Jesus' kingdom.

Hence the Old Testament vision of jubilean justice and the ethic of prophetic righteousness find fulfillment in Jesus' teachings and actions. The poor inherit the kingdom, the blind see, the lame walk, and the prisoners are released. Through Jesus' faithful stewardship of God's love, the poor and the outcasts found welcome and justice in God's kingdom.

The Love Command

Among the most basic and recurring ethical imperatives of the New Testament is the double love command, love for God and love for one's neighbor. The importance of this command to the distinctive character of Christian living can hardly be overestimated. It is found in every major New Testament writer and in a variety of forms.

The Gospels record several occasions in which Jesus set forth this command as the essence of Christian obligation. The one instance is Jesus' response to the scribe who asks which commandment is the greatest (Mk. 12:28-34; Matt. 22:34-40). Jesus' reply links together the important *Shema* text of Deuteronomy 6:4-5 and the ethical heart of the Holiness Code in Leviticus 19:18:

"The first is, 'Hear, O Israel:
The Lord our God, the Lord is one;
and you shall love the Lord your God
with all your heart, and with all your soul,
and with all your mind, and with all your strength.'
The second is this, 'You shall love your neighbor as yourself.'
There is no other commandment greater than these" (Mk.
    10:29-31).

Cutting through all the case laws and even the Mosaic decalogue, Jesus identifies these two commands as those upon which "depend all the law and the prophets" (Mt. 22:40).

Luke's use of this central imperative occurs in response to a lawyer's question, "Teacher, what shall I do to inherit eternal life?" After hearing the answer, the lawyer, "desiring to justify himself, said to Jesus, 'And who is my neighbor?'" Then follows the classic story of the Good Samaritan. What is thus unmistakably clear is that practical love which helps those in need is a prerequisite for inheriting life eternal. On the basis of the parallel content between the lawyer's initial question above and the question of the rich young ruler (Mk. 10:17-22; Mt. 19:16-22; Lk. 18:18-30), it is appropriate to consider Jesus' mandate for the ruler to sell his possessions and give to the poor as the practical expression of neighbor love (cf. Zacchaeus in Lk. 19:1-10).

Another aspect of the love command in the Gospels is Jesus' command to love not only the neighbor but also the enemy (Mt. 5:43-44). Climaxing the six Matthean antitheses, this command calls the Christian to indiscriminate expression of the perfect love of the heavenly Father (5:45-48). Jesus' love knows no limit, but even leads one to lay down one's life for others (Jn. 15:13).

The early Church considered Jesus' teaching on this matter to be normative as evidenced by the recurrence of this love command in the writings of Paul (Rom. 13:8-10; Gal. 5:14) and James (2:8). The practical expression of neighbor love is also incumbent upon the Christian:

> If your enemy is hungry, feed him; if he is thirsty, give him drink (Rom. 12:20a).

> But if anyone has the world's good and sees his brother in need, yet closes his heart against him, how does God's love abide in him? . . . Let us not love in word or speech but in deed and in truth (1 Jn 3:17-18).

The command to love is the biblical mandate to be stewards and ambassadors of that which describes God's own being, for God is love (1 Jn. 4:16b).[13] Such love mortifies selfishness and greed (Mk. 8:34-37; Gal. 5:16-26), looks out for the need of others (Gal. 6:1-2; Mt. 7:12; 1 Cor. 13), upbuilds the community in unity (Eph. 4:15-16), and enables faithful stewardship of all of life by fulfilling the will of God, the Father of Jesus Christ (Col. 3:12-17).

To live a life of love patterned after God's love in Christ (Eph. 5:1-2) is possible because, as the apostle Paul says, the believer has been "created after the likeness [*image*] of God in true righteousness and holiness" (Eph. 4:23). The *image* lost at the fall has been restored through Christ. Living out the love-command is thus a concrete expression of "being God's image" and thus fulfilling humankind's stewardship intended by the Creator.

Paul's Teachings on Giving

Scripture teaches the giving of money and material possessions to help those in need (Acts 11:29-30; 1 Cor. 16:1; 2 Cor. 8—9). As Holmes Rolston points out in his study of 2 Corinthians 8 and 9, the apostle Paul bases his appeal for giving on numerous considerations: (1) it proves the genuineness of one's love (8:8, 24); (2) it is an expression of God's grace (8:1ff.); (3) it expresses the fruit of the Spirit (8:7-8); (4) it follows the example of Jesus Christ who "though he was rich . . . became poor" (8:9); (5) it is to be guided by the vision of equality (8:13-15); (6) it is to be done liberally (8:2) and cheerfully (9:7), with assurance that the Lord will multiply the giver's resources (9:8-10); and (7) it is a ministry that meets needs of others ("saints"—9:12-13).[14]

While these Pauline teachings are commonly appealed to as instruction in Christian stewardship, Paul's willingness to risk death in order to share the relief gift with the needy in Jerusalem is more rarely noted. By comparing Romans 15 and Acts 20-21, it is clear that Paul's determination to go to Jerusalem at the end of his third missionary campaign, even despite Agabus' prophecy that he would be bound hand and foot (Acts 21:7-14), was motivated by his all-consuming desire to present the relief gift to the saints in Jerusalem (Rom. 15:31). Paul considered the gift to be an expression of the unity of the Gentile and Jewish Christians (15:27) and a vindication of his calling to be an apostle to the Gentiles (15:15-16, 31; cf. Eph. 3:1-13). Further, the only counsel ever given to Paul by the Jerusalem leaders was to remember the poor (Gal. 2:10)! As the scholarly study by Keith F. Nickle has shown,[15] relief for the poor in Jerusalem was a central concern of Paul's missionary work.

Final Judgment and Redemption

The several references in the Gospels to the concept of faithful and wise stewardship occur within the context of warnings of judgment. The parable of the wise and faithful steward in Luke 12:41-48 is one such instance. The larger context of the parable condemns covetousness, laying up treasures for oneself, and anxiety over worldly possessions—all within the shadow of warnings to be ready for the end either through death or final judgment (12:13-40). The parable itself is also one stressing readiness for the Master's unexpected arrival.

Similarly, Matthew's apocalyptic discourse (ch. 24) ends with the challenge: "Who then is the faithful and wise servant?" (24:45a). Then comes the parable of the wise and foolish virgins, the parable of the talents, and then the final judgment (ch. 25). The sheep welcomed into the kingdom to the Father's right hand are those who fed the hungry, gave drink to the thirsty, clothed the naked, and visited the prisoners. The goats who depart into everlasting punishment are those who didn't recognize and attend to the hungry, thirsty, naked, and imprisoned (Mt. 25:31-46). Christ himself is present in the poor, the hungry, the naked, and the imprisoned (25:40, 45). In the Sermon on the Mount, Jesus similarly calls his disciples to seek first the kingdom (6:33) and prepare for final judgment by doing the will of the Father. Power to do miracles will not guarantee salvation; rather the bearing of good fruit, building wisely upon rock, and doing the Father's will insures Jesus' welcome into the kingdom (Mt. 7:16-27).

Paul and James continue the teaching of Jesus. Paul's warning that "we shall all stand before the judgment seat of God" and "each of us shall give account of himself to God" is in the context of his admonition to consider the weaker brother, for "none of us lives to himself, and none of us dies to himself" (Rom. 14:8, 10, 12). Further, the work which one builds upon the foundation, the reception of Jesus Christ by grace through faith, will determine one's welfare in the judgment (1 Cor. 3:10-15). Similarly, James' eschatological admonition, "Establish your hearts, for the coming of the Lord is near" (5:8), is prefaced by numerous ethical injunctions: to lament the miseries of the rich, to shun passions which kindle war, to refuse faith that doesn't produce works, and to be doers of the word, not hearers only (chs. 1-5).

True it is that Christian salvation is never based upon works, but judgment *is,* in both the Old and New Testaments.[16] Whether based upon creation's call to responsible dominion, or the expected morality of the Old Testament covenant, or the kingdom justice proffered through Jesus Christ, God's norm for judgment consistently appeals to an ethical accountability—specifically, how faith expresses itself in love (Gal. 5:7) through deeds of helpfulness to the poor, hungry, naked, and oppressed. When one recognizes, however, that biblical thought regards righteousness and justice as virtually synonymous in the Old Testament, then justification for salvation and works of justice cannot be dichotomized in the New Testament. Justification and justice are one.

Paul's use of the term stewardship *(oikonomia)* in Ephesians 1:10 and 3:2 introduces also a correlation between Christian stewardship of God's grace (3:2) and God's stewardship of all time and creation (1:10). God's purpose is to unite all things in Jesus Christ. Hence the Christian's stewardship of grace, particularly the responsibility to share the Gospel with all people (Eph. 3:2ff). Hence, also, the vision that even the groaning creation will be liberated from the curses of the fall (Rom. 8:19ff.) and God's work of redemption will be complete. That which conquers all and promises ultimate victory is "the love of God in Jesus Christ our Lord" (Rom. 8:35-39). It appears, therefore, that works of love are the criteria of judgment, on the one hand, and the power of love is the promise of full and final redemption, on the other hand. In this pattern of divine initiative, human response, and divine sovereignty, humankind's stewardship of God's gifts and God's stewardship of all creation and mankind's response are inextricably entwined.

The Testimony of the Church Fathers

Because our modern Western cultural viewpoint takes for granted the right to private possessions, it is imperative that Christians test this assumption by the convictions of Christians in other periods of Church history. The testimony of the Church Fathers in the second through the fourth centuries shows two strands of

Biblical Sources of Stewardship

emphasis: one, predominant from 100 to 250 A.D., stressing sharing of goods and having possessions in common, and the other, predominant from 250 to 400 A.D., condemning wealth and regarding charity as justice.

Illustrative of the emphasis on sharing is the text from the Didache, an early Church manual representing the apostles' teaching and written c. 110 A.D. (location uncertain):

> Do not turn your back on the needy, but share everything with your brother and call nothing your own. For if you have what is eternal in common, how much more should you have what is transient (4:8).[17]

The Letter to Diognetus (c. 130 A.D.), in describing the life of the Christians, says: "They share their board with each other, but not their marriage bed" (5:7).[18] Bishop Dionysis of Corinth, writing c. 170 A.D., says:

> For this has been your custom from the beginning: to do good in diverse ways to all the brethren, and to send supplies to many churches in every city: now relieving the poverty of the needy, now making provision, by the supplies which you have been sending from the beginning, for brethren in the mines (forced labor imposed by the state).[19]

Clement of Alexandria (c. 200 A.D.) describes possessions "as the gifts of God" that are "more for the sake of the brethren than [one's] own." Further the Christian does not "carry them about in his soul, nor [allow them] to bind and circumscribe his life," and "is able with cheerful mind to bear their removal equally with their abundance."[20]

The early Church held that "holding goods in common" was a way of imitating God the Father, according to Cyprian of Carthage (c. 250 A.D.):

> For whatever is of God is common in our use, nor is anyone excluded from his benefits and his gifts, so as to prevent the whole human race from enjoying equally the divine goodness

and liberality. . . . In this example of equality, he who, as a possessor in the earth, shares his returns and his fruits with the fraternity, while he is common and just in his gratuitous bounties, is an imitator of God the Father.[21]

While more citations might be given, it is important to note that their frequency and range in time and location is such that modern Christians cannot dismiss the teaching as marginal. The pertinent question is whether this viewpoint does not in fact better accord with biblical teaching than does the modern Christian view that stresses acquisition of wealth and percentage giving.

The second strand of teaching predominates during the late third and fourth centuries, indicating no doubt that the Christians were at that time facing the temptation to acquire wealth and considerable private property. One of the most startling comments comes from St. Jerome (c. 390 A.D., monastery near Jerusalem):

And he very rightly said, "money of injustice," for *all riches come from injustice.* Unless one person has lost, another cannot find. Therefore I believe that the popular proverb is very true: "The rich person is either an unjust person or the heir of one."[23]

John Chrysostom (c. 400, patriarch of Constantinople) similarly says:

Tell me, how is it that you are rich? From whom did you receive your wealth? And he, whom did he receive it from? From his grandfather, you say, from his father. By climbing this genealogical tree are you able to show the justice of this possession? Of course you cannot; rather *its beginning and root have necessarily come out of injustice.* . . . Do not say, "I am spending what is mine; I am enjoying what is mine." In reality it is not yours but another's.[24]

Both Basil the Great (c. 365, bishop of Caesarea) and St. Ambrose (c. 380, bishop of Milan) indicate that possessions *belong* to those who need them:

When someone steals a man's clothes we call him *a thief.*
Should we not give the *same name to one who could clothe the
naked and does not?* The bread in your cupboard belongs to
the hungry man; the coat hanging unused in your closet belongs to the man who needs it; the shoes rotting in your closet
belong to the man who has no shoes; the money which you
hoard up belongs to the poor. [25]

You are not making a gift of your possessions to the poor man.
You are handing over to him what is his. [26]

Finally, the biblical view that humankind is called to be a
steward of what belongs to God, practicing justice and love, is
clearly enunciated by Ambrose:

God willed that this earth should be the common possession of
all and he offered its fruits to all. But avarice distributed the
rights of possession. [27]

Conclusion

For those who have ears to hear, biblical teaching speaks to
the contemporary issues of world hunger, rich nations vis à vis
poor nations, and the ecological crises. God created mankind to be
a steward of the earth's essential resources. "The earth and the
fullness thereof" belongs to its Creator, who made humankind in
the divine image, to represent *God's* ownership in the world, to
exert dominion in justice, and to enjoy the world's wealth by
accepting it as a common possession of all humanity. Herein does
love for God and for the neighbor find perfect expression.

NOTES

1. *The Interpreter's Dictionary of the Bible,* ed. by George Arthur
Buttrick, *et al.* (Nashville, Tenn.: Abingdon Press, 1962), Vol. IV, p. 443.
2. Quoted from Carl Kreider in Delton Franz, Carl Kreider, and

42   THE EARTH IS THE LORD'S

Andrew and Viola Shelley, *Let My People Choose: Christian Choice Regarding Poverty, Affluence, Standard of Living* (Scottdale, Pa.: Herald Press, 1969 and Newton, Kan.: Faith and Life Press, 1969), p. 77.

3. Gerhard von Rad, *Genesis: A Commentary*, trans. by John H. Marks (Philadelphia, Pa.: Westminster, 1961), pp. 57-58.

4. One stream of thought in early Christian writings identifies possessions or property as the cause of the first fraticide, based on exegesis of the name Cain (from *qana* = acquire and *qana'* = be envious). Because Cain presents an offering from his *own* labors in tilling the ground it is unacceptable. For discussion of this view see Martin Hengel, *Property and Riches in the Early Church: Aspects of a Social History of Early Christianity*, trans. by John Bowden (Philadelphia, Pa.: Fortress Press, 1974), pp. 1ff.

5. For a survey and analysis of these studies see Gerhard Hasel, *Old Testament Theology: Basic Issues in the Current Debate* (Grand Rapids, Mich.: Eerdmans, rev. ed., 1975), ch. IV.

6. Abraham J. Heschel, *The Prophets* (New York and Evanston: Harper and Row, 1962), pp. 3-4.

7. Philip F. Mulhern, *Dedicated Poverty: Its History and Theology* (Staten Island, N.Y.: Alba House, 1973), pp. 1-8.

8. *Ibid.*, pp. 7-11.

9. José Porfirio Miranda, *Marx and the Bible: A Critique of the Philosophy of Oppression*, trans. by John Eagleson (Maryknoll, New York: Orbis Books, 1974), pp. 93-94, 107, nn. 35-38.

10. Milo Kauffman, *Stewards of God* (Scottdale, Pa. and Kitchener, Ontario: Herald Press, 1975), p. 150.

11. John Howard Yoder, *The Politics of Jesus: Vicit Agnus Noster* (Grand Rapids, Mich.: Eerdmans, 1972), pp. 26-77.

12. For an extensive treatment of New Testament teaching regarding the poor, see Richard Batey, *Jesus and the Poor* (New York, et al.: Harper and Row, 1972).

13. Victor Paul Furnish in his helpful book, *The Love Command in the New Testament* (Nashville and New York: Abingdon Press), pp. 199-217, summarizes his findings under four main points: I. The New Testament commendation of love is formulated in a *command* to love. II. The Christian love command is the *sovereign* command of a *sovereign* Lord. III. By the love command a *community* of love is called into being and summoned to responsible action. IV. The command to love is, simultaneously, also a call to repentance and a proffer of forgiveness.

14. Holmes Rolston, *Stewardship in the New Testament Church: A Study in the Teachings of Saint Paul Concerning Christian Stewardship* (Richmond, Va.: John Knox Press, 1946), pp. 70-73.

15. Keith F. Nickle, *The Collection—A Study in Paul's Strategy* (London: SCM Press, 1965).

16. See also Ps. 62:12; Jer. 17:10; Mt. 16:27; 2 Cor. 5:10; 1 Pet. 1:17; Rev. 20:12; 22:12.

17. Cyril C. Richardson, ed., *Early Christian Fathers;* Vol. I: *Library*

of Christian Classics (Philadelphia, Pa.: The Westminster Press, 1953), p. 173.

18. *Ibid.*, p. 217.

19. Recorded in *Eusebius' Ecclesiastical History*, quoted from Hengel, *op. cit.*, p. 44.

20. In Clement's treatise entitled *The Rich Man's Salvation* (16:3), quoted from Hengel, *op. cit.*, p. 75.

21. From Cyprian's work entitled *On Good Works and Almsgiving* (25), quoted from Hengel, *op. cit.*, p. 80.

22. E.g., Aristides' *Apologia* 15:7f; writing c. 125 A.D. from Athens (Hengel, *op. cit.*, pp. 42-43); *First Apology of Justin* 67 (*Early Christian Fathers*, p. 287); Cyprian of Carthage in Hengel, *op. cit.*, p. 81; and Octavius 36:5 (*The Octavius of Marcus Minucius Felix, Ancient Christian Writers*, vol. 39, trans. by G. W. Clarke [New York, N. Y.: Newman Press, 1974], p. 119).

23. "Carta 120," *Patrologiae cursus . . . Series latina* (hereafter PL) 22, col. 984. This and the following quotations are found in José Miranda, *op. cit.*, p. 15.

24. "In 1 Tim.," PG (*graeca*) 61, col. 86.

25. "Homily on Luke," PG 31, col. 277.

26. "De Nabuthe," PL 14, col. 747.

27. PL 15, col. 1303.

The Ethics of Stewardship

William J. Byron

This essay in theological ethics is grounded in supernatural faith and focused on human character. Men and women of all ages in every age of creation are children of God. They are adopted children, redeemed, which is to say "bought back" by God in Christ. The fundamental law of adoption is gratitude. And gratitude, in the perspective of theological ethics, is the ground of obligation.

The Mystery of God's Graciousness

The mystery of God's graciousness to us in Christ is presented by St. John in language that stresses divine initiative and human undeservedness. "Anyone who fails to love can never have known God, because God is love. God's love for us was revealed when God sent into the world his only Son so that we could have life through him; this is the love I mean: not our love for God, but God's love for us when he sent his Son to be the sacrifice that takes our sins away. . . . We are to love, then, because he loved us first" (1 Jn. 4:8-10, 19).

The initiative is all one-sided—"He loved us first." We had no claim, no right to that redeeming love. All we had was need. God's gracious favor toward us—divine grace, in other words—is unexplainable from our side. It is, therefore, a mystery.

St. Paul makes the same point when he writes: "The love of God has been poured into our hearts by the Holy Spirit which has been given us. We were still helpless when, at his appointed moment, Christ died for sinful men. It is not easy to die even for a good man—though of course for someone really worthy, a man might be prepared to die—but what proves that God loves us is that Christ died for us while we were still sinners" (Rom. 5:5-7). Mathematically expressed, the ratio here would be 1:0.

Similarly, God's graciousness manifests itself to us in *material* terms. And again, the ratio is 1:0. We have no prior claim, no antecedent title to possess the gifts of creation, all of which are summed up in a single category, "the land." Gifted with the land, we are bound to be grateful. Grateful for the land, we are obligated to preserve it, share it and use it in accordance with God's plan.

Stewardship: Fidelity to God's Gift

Stewardship is a traditional category which touches both the gift dimension and the moral obligation associated with people and "the land." I am not speaking of the new or "promised" land to which God calls his chosen people. I am speaking of the land— material creation—given by God to our care and for our use. Stewardship says that no human person owns anything absolutely; everything we possess we hold in trust. The conditions of that trust are set by the Creator who "entrusts" to our care varying proportions of material creation. An ethic of stewardship concerns itself with fidelity to, and violations of, that trust.

The unethical steward is the person who violates that trust (1) by neglecting to care for that which has been entrusted; (2) by destroying without adequate reason the substance of that which has been entrusted; or (3) by appropriating or assigning to oneself the exclusive use of that which has been entrusted, and doing so in a way which denies the legitimate claims of others. An unethical steward is one who enriches himself or herself on that which has been entrusted, at the expense of those (including future generations) for whom the trust is held. The unethical steward is characterized by insensitivity, pride, avarice and greed. The ethical steward exhibits a character, the internal source of external behavior, which is compassionate, trustworthy, humble, self-sacrificing. These qualities are descriptive of the person of Christ. These virtues are possible in us only through the grace of Christ. The contradictory vices are sins or sinful tendencies which await the healing power of the grace of Christ.

Private Property: Need for a Fresh Perspective

It is late, but not, of course, too late for Christian ethicists and theologians to reflect on private property as an occasion of contemporary sin and unethical conduct. This would be yet another approach to the exaggerated egocentricity which is personal sin and the collective depersonalization, damage and disregard which describe social sin. This approach would not be the only approach, just a fresh perspective necessitated by the evidence of sinfulness in our times (the extremes of wealth, poverty, human oppression, starvation, and the unjust exploitation of both resources and persons). Personal and social sin must be examined today through the window of private property.

St. Augustine specified slavery, government and private property as results of original sin. St. Thomas Aquinas regarded the institution of private property as an accommodation to the state of the human race after the fall. As one of the principles around which human societies can be organized, private property is seen by Aquinas as a form of social organization which offers a realistic expectation that property will be preserved for the service of the community. Aristotle before him noted in the *Politics*, "That which is common to the greatest number has the least care bestowed upon it." Compare your own conduct in a public park and your private garden, in a rented automobile and your family car. Sinful human beings all, we have an on-going moral problem in containing our disordered self-interest. As Edmund Burke once remarked, "Every man that is ruined is ruined on the side of his natural propensities." Those propensities must be held in check.

Since the possession of private property appeals to our self-interest, the institution of private property represents a workable, although risky, way of preserving "the land." But preservation is only part of the task of stewardship. Sharing the land and using it for the benefit of the community require equal attention. Traditional moral analysis would grant to those in real need, and to those who have been unjustly denied access to the land, the right to override another's right of private ownership. By refusing to share, or by denying necessary access to the community, or by unreasonably exploiting, for motives of personal enrichment at the expense of others, the land and those who labor on it, the private owner reveals himself or herself to be unethical in the conduct of stewardship.

Motives for an Ethic of Stewardship

The foundation in wisdom for ethical stewardship requires a recognition and practical acceptance of the one-to-zero ratio that describes the relationship of God and the human person.

With profound insight and moving expression, Mahatma Gandhi once said, "There comes a time when an individual becomes irresistible and his action becomes all-pervasive in its effect. This comes when he reduces himself to zero." The ethics of stewardship challenge all who people the land—owners, users, possessors and the dispossessed—to relate to one another as zero-to-zero. Not doormat-to-doormat, but zero-to-zero in recognition and acceptance of the one-to-zero ratio that describes both the economy of grace and the gratuity of material creation.

Attitudinal change will be a necessary forerunner to any realization of this ethical ideal. An attitude is a tendency toward action, and behind the tendency there will always be a motive. Abundant motives are available for incorporation into a contemporary ethic of stewardship.

On the one hand, environmental and ecological data are registering concern among those whose eyes (although burning) can still see, and whose ears (although ringing) can still hear. Air, water, soil and noise pollution are outdistancing control measures. Non-renewable resources are being rapidly depleted. New technology is not keeping pace; population growth in the poor two-thirds of the world and consumption growth in the affluent one-third of the world pit people against resources as well as people against people along lines of division on "the land." These emerging lines suggest that the land, if managed in a way contrary to the ethics of stewardship, has the potential in our day of becoming a battleground between rich and poor. Personal and collective self-interest perceived in terms of survival (the ultimate natural motive) would, one might expect, nudge us toward remedial or preventative action. Prior to action, however, there must be attitudinal change. We simply cannot continue the attitude that "what is mine is mine absolutely and I can do with it as I wish." Nor can we afford to continue to sustain the attitude that "my money entitles me to consume or control on my own terms as much as my money will buy."

Shame is an excellent natural motive for correcting imbalances resulting from the neglect of stewardship responsibilities. The typical American will not accept guilt as a fair verdict in judgment of his or her role in the world food crisis. But such a person can legitimately feel shame to be so well off in a world where innocent others suffer so much poverty. Ashamed at my disinterest and disregard for the poor, and embarrassed to admit that I co-exist on "the land" with needy people whom I neither know nor try to help, I might recall my own original zero status before the sole owner of "the land" and decide to do something.

On the other hand, there are divine commands, religious traditions, inspired writings and theological developments, none of which need to be catalogued here, which make it plain that "the earth is the Lord's and the fullness thereof" (Ps. 24:1), and that we who possess any portion of the earth's resources are obliged to "love one another" (1 Jn. 4:12). Specifically, our tradition will never stop bothering us with the disturbing question posed by St. John: "If a man who was rich enough in this world's goods saw that one of his brothers was in need, but closed his heart to him, how could the love of God be living in him?" (1 Jn. 3:17). And without the love of God, as our theology of grace reminds us, we are nothing, zero.

Signs of Hope

In the secular sphere, analysts are noting a shift in ideas and attitudes that underlie our economic institutions, thus making the traditional foundations for those institutions less secure. Classical economic analysis regarded human labor (along with land and capital) as a "factor" of production. "Economic man" was presumed to act only in ways conducive to the maximization of personal utility and satisfaction. Today we have all but broken away from a "value-free" economics. We see no longer an "economic man" but a human person interacting with other human persons as well as material wealth in an economic system. The system itself, regarded by all as standing in need of improvement, is seen to be a complex but consciously coordinated network of activities rather than a constellation of blind forces operating with the blessing of Adam Smith's "invisible hand." Most, but not all, who live within the American economic system see evolution and reform as capable of shaping that system toward greater sensitivity and responsiveness to human values. Some, representing a significant minority, see revolution and replacement of the system as the only way of correcting the human disvalues and curbing the abuses of economic power at home and abroad made possible by the material successes of the American economic system. With an eye on changing values within the American economic system, George C. Lodge notes the emergence of *The New American Ideology,* the title of his 1975 book, which sees individualism, competition and exaggerated private property-interests all on the decline. Institutions whose legitimacy rests on these "old ideas" are in trouble. On the rise in the American mind is an attitude, a value, a tendency toward action which Lodge calls "communitarianism." "America," writes Lodge, "now appears to be heading into a return to the communal norms of both the ancient and medieval world."

This does not mean a return to pre-capitalist forms of economic organization, nor does it herald the arrival of socialism or even communism as the way to solve the problem of irresponsible private ownership—i.e., private ownership that is not responsive to genuine human need. If private owners admit that they own nothing absolutely, and that everything they possess has been entrusted to them by the one Lord and Owner of it all, then a biblically-based humanism will temper our sinful tendencies to use, produce and distribute wealth as if it really belonged to us.

The Christian, in the view of Teilhard de Chardin, must be "the most attached and detached of men" in his or her dealings with both the earth and the fullness thereof. God intends this to be the case. Stewardship is the controlling category needed to keep this tension creative. The ethics of stewardship, today both under-developed theoretically and, as a result, underapplied practically, offers a vehicle for moving a great moral tradition forward toward incorporation in the ideology which is newly emerging in America. There are signs of a new receptivity in America to the notion of Christian stewardship at the very moment when private property is emerging as a central issue in ethical discourse. That discourse will be better informed if it can presuppose the practice of the kind of *prayer* (recall that this is an essay in theological ethics, grounded in supernatural faith) that can be translated into a life-style, a life-style consistent with the principles of good stewardship.

Such prayer will acknowledge that a one-to-zero ratio exists not only in the order of grace but also in the order of creation. It will be contemplative of creation but not stop there; it will move through nature to contemplate the author of nature. This prayer will be characterized by a sense of awe, and the awe will lead to gratitude. From gratitude will spring obligation.

For prayer like this to become a life-style, it cannot be episodic. It must be habitual. Such prayer will shape one's attitude toward material creation. And from a new attitude there will emerge a new ethics of stewardship over the same material creation.

Adam Smith, Milton Friedman, and Christian Economics

Howard Richards

Ethics, which deals with right and wrong, and economics, which deals with money, must, it would seem, have something to do with one another. Frequently it appears that what they have to do with each other is that the latter prevents us from doing what the former declares to be our plain duty. Ethics tells us that it is a duty to work; economics tells us that full employment is highly unlikely. Ethics tells us that we should ship our surplus grain overseas to share it with those in need; economics tells us that food gifts depress prices, thereby discouraging the farmers of the countries to which the gifts are sent. Ethics says that we should care for those who are unable to care for themselves; economics says that social welfare programs are inflationary. Ethics calls for an equitable tax structure; economics replies that heavy taxation of wealth will result in "failure to provide sufficient replacement to maintain capital intact."[1]

In principle, ethics and economics should always agree. Ethics is the study of right conduct, and since conduct in business and industry is a part or subdivision of human conduct generally, economics ought to be a part or subdivision of ethics. That is the traditional concept—that economics is to ethics as part is to whole; it is the view that characterized our Judaeo-Greek-Christian civilization for two thousand years, almost up to the publication of Adam Smith's *Wealth of Nations* in 1776. In order to emphasize the contrast between modern and the traditional viewpoints, I have in the preceding paragraph purposely exaggerated—but it is an exaggeration with a meaningful point, for it is typical of our times that the clergyman plays the role of the spinner of castles in the air in the realm of what-ought-to-be-but-never-will-be, while the economist justifies Carlyle's description of economics as "the dismal science" by playing the role of harbinger of bad news.

"I'd like to help you out. Which way did you come in?" A glance at the history of the stormy relationship of ethics and economics may help us to understand how we got where we are, and to chart where to go from here.

Adam Smith

An essential difference between Christian economics and the secular school founded by Adam Smith lies in their respective concepts of justice. The premises of the religious view are that the earth belongs to God, and that we are commanded by God to love and serve one another. It follows that private property is good because and insofar as it is a useful means for the achievement of proper objectives. The economy was made for man, not man for the economy.

The traditional doctrine is expressed, for example, in the *Summa Theologica* of St. Thomas Aquinas:

> The temporal goods which God grants us, are ours as to the ownership, but as to the use of them, they belong not to us alone but also to such others as we are able to succour out of what we have over and above our needs.[2]

Aquinas' doctrine is not merely that it is praiseworthy to give to the poor out of what is ours, but rather that those in need have ownership rights in our surplus. Aquinas explicitly considers a question which Adam Smith also explicitly considers, namely whether giving of one's "own" to aid those in need is a duty of justice or merely an act of liberality. Thomas answers that it is a duty of justice, employing Aristotle's concept of distributive justice in affirming that the act of giving is merely granting to the needy person his just due:

Now each man's own is that which is due to him according to
equality of proportion. Therefore, the proper act of justice is
nothing else than to render to each his own.[3]

Adam Smith gives the opposite answer to the same question. I
quote Smith:

Mere justice is, upon most occasions, but a negative virtue,
and only hinders us from hurting our neighbor. The man who
barely abstains from violating either the person or the estate,
or the reputation, of his neighbors, has surely very little positive merit. He fulfills, however, all the rules of what is pecu-
liarly called justice, and does every thing which his equals can
with propriety force him to do, or which they can punish him
for not doing. We may often fulfill all the rules of justice by
sitting still and doing nothing.[4]

To share of one's surplus to attend to those in need is not, for
Smith, an act of justice, but rather one of benevolence, and benevolence is not a duty. Justice, properly so called, consists of a strict
and reverential respect for the rights of private property, without
which society as Smith conceives it would be destroyed. Smith
compares justice to grammar and benevolence to style. The rules
of justice, like grammar, are strict and bind everyone to the most
exact respect for property rights. The rules of benevolence, like
style, are loose and are left to the discretion of the donor.

The major significance of Smith's work does not lie, however,
in its ethics, but in its tendency to discuss economic questions as if
economics were a natural science, thereby short-circuiting questions of right and wrong altogether. Smith's work is an unfortunate
example of the eighteenth-century vogue for following the lead of
Sir Isaac Newton, who achieved spectacular progress in physics
and astronomy by avoiding the attribution of human qualities (such
as "final causes," i.e., purposes) to the motions of physical objects,
treating them instead as motions due to forces (i.e., to "efficient
causes"). Newton's method is more defensible than Smith's, for
Newton treats things as things, and things are things, whereas

Smith treats persons as things, and persons are not things.

For example, in discussing the evasion of certain Spanish tariff and customs laws, Smith describes the laws as a "dam" and the desire to violate it as a "stream of water."[5] The king of Spain would have classified smugglers together with scamps and sinners rather than together with stones, stars, and streams. Smith might have claimed that smugglers should be excused from punishment, since he did not share the opinion of the Spanish authorities that restrictions on international trade foster the moral and material welfare of a kingdom, but he saved himself the trouble of justifying their conduct because he described them as if they were natural forces—a class of entities to whose actions the predicates "right" and "wrong" do not apply.

It was by using metaphors from the natural sciences that Smith became the most important of the founders of economics as we know it today, insofar as economics describes commerce in a way that assumes (by the very fact of describing it with metaphors appropriate for natural phenomena) that commerce is like the phenomena studied by the natural sciences. Thus Marshall held that economic competition is simply an instance of the biological law of the survival of the fittest.[6] He explained the institution of the market by comparing it, at what he called equilibrium, to a stone balanced on the end of a needle; Jevons explained the same concept through the theory of the lever, and Edgworth compared it to the behavior of a gas under pressure.[7] For these economists, supply and demand play the role of "forces," and the point where supply and demand are in equilibrium is one where the two forces compensate one another.

Milton Friedman

Professor Milton Friedman of the University of Chicago, a contemporary follower of Adam Smith, believes that a correct relationship between ethics (i.e., policy) and economics requires the following premise:

Any policy conclusion necessarily rests on a prediction about the consequences of doing one thing rather than another, a prediction that must be based—implicitly or explicitly—on positive economics.[8]

In other words, the task of economics is to establish principles of cause and effect, which will enable Christians and other ladies and gentlemen of good will to make good faith choices among the options open to them in the light of scientific knowledge of what the consequences of choosing any given option will be.

When Friedman explains how the theoretical principles that enable the economist to predict consequences are to be discovered by research, one suspects that the Chicago professor is haunted by the ghost of Sir Isaac Newton. For example:

A hypothesis or theory consists of an assertion that certain forces are, and by implication others are not, important for a particular class of phenomena and a specification of the manner of action of the forces it asserts to be important.[9]

Some of us do not believe that the metaphor of interaction of forces provides an adequate account of the conduct of persons—but for the sake of brevity I will not argue that point here, but only observe that if the Newtonian persuasion be accepted for the sake of argument, then Friedman must at least concede that economics studies complex phenomena where many imperfectly understood factors are at work.

Right away we note that economics is not like physics, and if Friedman asks that his opinions on economics be accorded the respect that we pay to the opinions on physics of a physicist, we must deny him that honor. In physics (more precisely, in Newtonian mechanics) a theory is refuted if a crucial prediction fails to come true, because the physicist is supposed to know what all the relevant factors are and to take them into account. If his prediction fails, his theory or his calculations or both are wrong.[10] On the other hand, even though Milton Friedman expressed confidence in the middle 1960's that unemployment would not in the foreseeable future be a serious problem in America, we do not say that therefore his theory has been tested and refuted—we allow him to excuse himself. He is allowed to say that he could not have been expected to take into account that the government would engage in all that tomfoolery or that OPEC would raise the price of oil, and we accept that sort of excuse because we are aware of the difficulties that students of complex phenomena labor under.

The expectation that Friedman's economics will yield accurate predictions of the consequences of an array of policy options is a mirage which disappears as one approaches it. More than other economists, he posits simple explanations for complex phenomena, but more than other economists he allows himself leeway for explaining away facts which contradict his theories. The justification for these harsh words will be found in the footnote and in the works there cited. [11]

As was the case with Adam Smith, Milton Friedman (the economist) is a good friend of Milton Friedman (the moral philosopher). In the intervening two hundred years, however, there has been considerable regress, so that while Smith held only that the precepts of the good steward, who manages God's property to serve his children, were not morally obligatory, Friedman holds that they are neither workable nor desirable. He writes:

> Unless the behavior of businessmen in some way or other approximated behavior consistent with the maximization of returns, it seems unlikely that they would remain in business for long. [12]

This doctrine is a long way from the Bible:

> When you reap the harvest in your land, you shall not reap right into the edges of your field, neither shall you glean the fallen ears. You shall leave them for the poor and for the alien. I am the Lord your God (Lev. 23:22).

The real world is considerably different from Friedman's theory, and in the real world it is easy to find successful businesses whose primary objective is to serve the public, businesses which include providing employment and promoting environmental quality among their corporate objectives, and even businesses which donate all their profits to charitable foundations. Friedman (the moral philosopher) disapproves of these deviations from the assumptions about the behavior of businesspeople which Friedman (the economist) postulates. Friedman (the economist) finds that intense competition is an effective technique for driving weak or generous businesses to bankruptcy, and he recommends an open door for imports in order to provide foreign competition to augment the pressure of local competition.[13] Friedman (the moral philosopher) believes that in the long run everyone will be better off if we put our faith in competition and shy away from conscience.

It is tempting to dismiss Friedman on the ground that from mistaken premises (materialism and individualism) only mistaken conclusions can come. Dismal in: dismal out. But he must be at least partly right; competition, within the rules of the game fixed by law, must be one way, and sometimes the best way, to guide economic behavior. Furthermore, it is instructive to examine the way in which his research in economics and his ethical convictions reinforce each other, as I shall try to illustrate in the following analysis of his findings concerning the impact of the minimum wage laws on the employment opportunities of the poor.

Friedman's findings are bad news for the poor. Minimum wage laws tend to price labor out of the market, creating unemployment. It follows that the choice for many workers is an unhappy one: work at substandard wages (without minimum wage laws) or unemployment (with minimum wage laws). The poor lose either way.

Before accepting this conclusion at face value one might raise the question whether the consequences of the minimum wage laws is the sort of thing that can be studied scientifically at all. In a complex system where it is supposed that many factors are at work, it is in principle difficult to sort out the effect of a change in a single variable. If, for example, a minimum wage is enacted and employment goes up, one might argue that it would have gone up anyway. If it goes down one might argue that it would have gone down anyway.

Friedman's answer to this objection is that he has been able to distinguish the impact of the minimum wage from the effects of other factors, either by holding those other factors constant (in a manner analogous to the controlled experiment of the natural sciences) or by estimating their effects separately and making allowances for them. As long as we continue to accept for the sake of argument (but contrary to our convictions) the frame of reference provided by the Newtonian persuasion, we must grant that Friedman's answer is a good one. But notice that his answer gives us a clearer focus on what his evidence tends to show. It does not show that minimum wage laws cause unemployment. What it shows is that minimum wages cause unemployment, *other things being equal*. What follows from this is decisive: if there is to be hope for the poor, those other things must become unequal. Friedman has helped us to see that the only economic programs that are likely to be acceptable from an ethical point of view will be programs that deal simultaneously with a large number of variables.

One could propose a comprehensive economic policy that would achieve both minimum wages and high employment. Friedman is aware that such policies are possible, and he opposes them.[14] It is at this point that Friedman (the moral philosopher) comes to the rescue of Friedman (the economist). It is necessary to assume the property rights and market "forces" of the status quo, and to change one factor at a time, for it to be plausible for Friedman (the economist) to posit simple explanations for complex phenomena. Conveniently enough, Friedman (the moral philosopher) is convinced that comprehensive policies designed to "bring any real constitution as near . . . as possible [to the ideal] by such gentle alterations and innovations as may not give too great disturbance to society"[15] should not be pursued.

I can now rest my case because I have illustrated the proposition that ethical critiques of economic institutions cannot be short-circuited by pretending that economics is a science. For the sake of completeness, however, I shall discuss briefly some of Friedman's reasons for believing that his rather extreme version of free market capitalism is the best of all possible institutional arrangements. In the first place, he takes a dualistic view of the alternatives, claiming:

Fundamentally, there are only two ways of coordinating the

economic activities of millions. One is central direction involving the use of coercion—the technique of the army and of the modern totalitarian state. The other is voluntary cooperation of individuals—the technique of the market place.[16]

In this manner, he simplifies his argument, since all he needs to point out is that the coercion of the army and the modern totalitarian state is the less eligible option, in order to draw the conclusion that the institutions he favors represent the better of the two possibilities. Second, Friedman's study of history convinces him that the adoption of moderate economic measures[17] tends to lead to dictatorship, while liberty flourishes under pure capitalism. Missioners who have spent time in the third world will not be likely to agree with Friedman's analysis of historical trends, for in those countries there is a different trend, in which nations which develop mixed economies with middle-of-the-road approaches to social problems tend to get much higher marks on respect for human rights and liberties than those nations which follow Professor Friedman's economic prescriptions. Third, he claims that policies of the kind he opposes are likely to be bungled and abused by all-too-human corporate managers and civil servants.[18] Here one can agree with Friedman's conservative appraisal of human nature, while reserving the right to comment that by bringing the human propensity to sin into the picture Friedman has finally gotten to the heart of the matter, to the point where he should have begun. All of the spiritual resources of the several religious traditions, and, more broadly, of culture, are needed to compensate for human frailty. At this point one must abandon the Newtonian persuasion—barely tolerable as a methodology, it is disastrous as a world view. For by treating economic activity in terms of the interplay of forces instead of the conduct of persons, it excludes from consideration the human qualities on which our hopes for a better world principally depend.

NOTES

1. A. C. Pigou, *The Economics of Welfare* (London: Macmillan, 1929), p. 52. ". . . the demise of the last capital item will certainly have

been preceded by that of the 'last man'" (*ibid.*, p. 53).

2. St. Thomas Aquinas, *Summa Theologica* (London: Burns Oates & Washbourne Ltd., 1922), II, II Q. 32, art. 5, ad. 2.

3. *Ibid.*, II, II, Q. 58, art. 11.

4. Adam Smith, *Theory of the Moral Sentiments* (London: Henry G. Bohn, 1861), p. 117.

5. Adam Smith, *The Wealth of Nations*, Modern Library edition (New York: Random House, 1937), pp. 478-479.

6. Alfred Marshall, *Principles of Economics*, 8th ed. (London: Macmillan, 1930), p. 597. It would follow that Marshall should change his theory now that biologists have modified the theory of evolution to include the crucial role of cooperation (symbiosis). See S. M. Henry (ed.), *Symbiosis* (New York: Academic Press, 1966).

7. Gérard Grellet, *Nouvelle Critique de l'Economie Politique* (Paris: Calmann-Levy, 1976), pp. 79-80.

8. Milton Friedman, "The Methodology of Positive Economics," in *Essays in Positive Economics* (Chicago: University of Chicago Press, 1953), p. 5. Cited hereafter as *Methodology*. By "positive" economics he means economics not mixed with value judgments.

9. *Ibid.*, p. 24.

10. A more detailed treatment would show that my account of the testing of hypotheses in physics is too simple. However, it is defensible to make a sharp distinction between physics and economics. See E. Grunberg, "Notes on the Verifiability of Economic Laws," *Philosophy of Science*, Vol. 24 (1957), pp. 337-348.

11. See, e.g., Paul Samuelson, "Report Card for the Federal Reserve: Monetarism vs. the Majority" in his *Economics*, 8th ed. (New York: McGraw-Hill, 1970). For an example of reluctance to recognize facts not predicted by theory, see the debate between Milton Friedman and Robert V. Roosa, *The Balance of Payments: Free versus Fixed Exchange Rates* (Washington: American Enterprise Institute, 1967), e.g., pp. 106-107. Friedman takes the view that it is not necessary for economics to describe correctly the way that business people really behave. Friedman, *Methodology*, p. 14. For a criticism of that paradoxical thesis, see R. M. Cyert and E. Grunberg, "Assumption, Prediction, and Explanation in Economics," in Richard M. Cyert and James G. March (eds.), *A Behavioral Theory of the Firm* (Englewood Cliffs: Prentice-Hall, 1963), pp. 298ff. He also holds that predictions need not be accurate "because the extra accuracy it [i.e. a general theory] yields may not justify the extra cost" (Friedman, *Methodology*), p. 18. In the end, the determinants of the acceptance of an economic theory turn out to be sociological, since they depend indirectly on what schools of thought are in fact influential among professional economists, according to Friedman, *Methodology*, p. 23. And on the competence of the economist being certified by the "right" kind of training, cf. Friedman, *Methodology*, p. 25. See generally E. Rotwein, "On 'The Methodology of Positive Economics,'" *Quarterly Journal of Eco-*

nomics, Vol. 73 (1959), pp. 554-575. See also William Poole and Elinda Kornblith, "The Friedman-Meiselman CMC Paper: New Evidence on an Old Controversy," *American Economic Review,* Vol. 63 (1973), p. 908. "These findings indicate that none of the single equation models predict the future very well": *ibid.,* p. 916.

12. Friedman, *Methodology,* p. 22.

13. His rationale for the indiscriminate promotion of international trade is the division of labor according to the principle of comparative advantage. By adopting the ideal of division of labor he rejects the ideal of self-sufficiency, either in the latter's limited form of energy independence or in a wider form. The principle of comparative advantage endorses the ideal that we should buy from whoever produces goods most cheaply. We would behave much differently if we preferred those suppliers who produce goods under decent working conditions.

14. Milton Friedman, "Lerner on the Economics of Control," in *op. cit.,* n. 8.

15. David Hume, quoted by Dugald Stewart in his introduction to *op. cit.,* n. 4 *supra,* p. lviii.

16. Milton Friedman, *Capitalism and Freedom* (Chicago: University of Chicago Press, 1962), p. 13.

17. *Ibid., passim.*

18. *Ibid.* and *op. cit.* n. 14.

Stewardship:
The Feminine Perspective

Doris Donnelly

Stewardship has to do with wealth and resources held in trust for others. As such, it deals with the right order of and attitudes toward possessions; it is concerned with the right uses of power; and it is ultimately involved with the constructive, imaginative and proportionate use of the good things of this world.

I am of the opinion that a feminine perspective on the question of stewardship and the contiguous issues of justice, power, possessions and accountability could enhance our understanding of stewardship. My reasons are based on three methodological decisions:

1. On the subject of possessions, I believe we might be well served by attending to the patriarchal religious context of Judaism in which *women,* along with land and cattle, *were themselves regarded as possessions.* Along with other Near Eastern religions, Judaism allowed women to be regarded as "property" to be dealt with and disposed of by men who were their stewards.

2. This optic, I suggest, allows women to comment from an unusual vantage point ("from the inside," as it were) on the issues of justice and the right uses of power/influence because of the injustice and abuses of power inherent in their experience. It is another way of saying: "If the earth could speak, if the land could verbalize how it is experiencing the exploitation of peoples, what would it say?"—and I am suggesting that if we listen to what women are saying, they may offer us some answers.

3. I further believe that women's current quest for liberation helps women to identify more empathetically with the oppressed—with those in want and in need. The contemporary

woman and the woman of Israel in pre-Christian times are "sisters." Both "sets" offer models of persons who are able to be compassionate to the hurts of other wounded persons and are able to inform an intelligent perspective on how a coalition of persons can be formed so that its needs be heard.

Given these methodological assumptions, our focus can be refined by reflection on three terms gaining ample currency in the women's movement. These terms are *dignity, productivity* and *justice*.

Background: Woman as Property

We are not without documentation to support the fact that woman's position in the Old Testament was subordinate and menial, often unprotected by man's law in a man's world. Very simply, woman was often not treated with the dignity to which she was entitled.

The Near Eastern family of historical times was patriarchal both in character and organization. Like the king who ruled over his realm, so did the *paterfamilias* dominate his household. He was, as the Western Semites called him, the *baal* (owner) of his wives and children. There were moments in history when the state fought an unceasing battle to restrict the absolute authority of the father who, within his own domain, had the physical power and the legal right to treat his wife and children as he pleased and even to dispose of them as he saw fit. Unfortunately, little progress on behalf of women was made.

The laws of marriage, divorce and inheritance further strengthened men's control and women's servitude and increased the extent to which she was regarded as property. One type of marriage, in particular, that fostered this bondage was the Levirate marriage. This institution had its roots in primitive society where a woman was acquired for wifehood by the head of the family for one of its members. She was, of course, given as a wife to one man, but when that man died, the widow remained the property of the group and was given as a wife to another male member of the family.

Ancient Near Eastern marriages were notoriously dissoluble.

As is evident from Hosea 2:2, a man could divorce his wife at any time by pronouncing the simple formula "She is not my wife; I am not her husband," and the marriage was thereby dissolved. While a man could divorce his wife at his pleasure, a woman was threatened with dire results if she wished to exercise the same privilege.

Adultery was a crime when committed by the betrothed or married woman but not when committed by the husband. The woman's partner in the act of adultery was considered guilty because he trespassed the husband's property: he stole a man's wife, and theft, as we know, was punishable by death.

Further, since daughters married strangers and thus cut themselves off from their family, only sons could inherit the paternal estate. It was sons who perpetuated the family name (2 Sam. 14:7). The principle that daughters did not inherit was maintained in the Old Testament even in the exceptional case of the daughter of Zelophehad. The decision laid down was that where there were no sons, daughters inherited provided that they married men of their father's family (Num. 27:11; 36:1-2; see also 1 Chr. 23:22).

I

DIGNITY: THE QUALITY OF WHAT WE POSSESS IN TRUST

While the coming of Jesus dignified the status of woman, the Church Fathers and medieval theologians soon succeeded in neutralizing the gains that Jesus made for her. Thus, the liberation impetus for contemporary woman's drive is similar to the liberation impetus for women in pre-Christian times—a quest for *dignity*.

To clarify the notion of dignity, I should like to refer to the distinctions made by Herbert W. Richardson in *Toward an American Theology*.

1. Dignity is the basis for authority. It is what gives weight to words, i. e., turns them into commands.

2. Dignity is the basis for tragedy. It is what gives life meaning and redeems it from triviality.

3. Dignity is the basis for meaning. It is not identical with meaning, since meaning is related to essence and is grasped by understanding. Even though life may have meaning, it may not have dignity. (p. 123)

What should interest us here is the second proposition —that dignity is the basis for tragedy. Aristotle suggests that for a tragedy to be genuine it must concern a person of intrinsic importance or weight. This is so because what happens to a person who has no dignity will not be of significance to anyone at all and thus will not be tragic. An added element of interest is that if a person lacks all sense of his/her own personal dignity, then he/she will not even care what happens to him/herself.

In this vein, it is interesting that one of the rallying cries of women (as well as the hungry) is that they be treated with or accorded "dignity"—that is, that those with dignity confer dignity upon them. This process would accord women/the poor/the oppressed *weight* so that their sufferings would be of some significance, so that their situation—their anxieties, their pain, their joys—*would matter* and be of some consequence. To continue to withhold dignity from the hungry, to treat them with disdain, to ignore them is to say that they are incapable of jolting our sensibilities and that it does not matter what happens to them. It is this callous way of reasoning that provokes statements which suggest that a life is a trivial consideration in some nations and that the death of a child in Bangladesh or Rhodesia or Israel should not evoke the pathos of its parents as an analogous situation in the United States would. An organization like Bread for the World reinforces the dignity of the hungry by taking their plight seriously, by raising it to the level of conscience and by urging us to make decisions in light of our freedom.

My point here is to suggest that the issue of dignity is essential to the question of stewardship and that we may learn about the articulation and passion for dignity from the pilgrimage that women are making. Theirs is precisely a striving for a share of dignity.

II
PRODUCTIVITY: HOW TO RELATE TO WHAT WE HAVE

Women's productivity in the Old Testament and even now has been closely associated with her childbearing capacity. The measure of her womanhood was calculated by the numbers of her children and particularly by the numbers of her sons. To be ful-

filled, accomplished, satisfied, a woman (then and now) has been
urged to give birth.

Paradoxically, one of the first experiences a mother has after
giving birth is an understanding that the child she has just birthed is
a gift held in trust for others and that her role after the birth of her
child is to encourage that person to full independence. The point is
that any mother knows that a child does not "belong" to her, that
she does not "possess" a child. Healthy maternity would have
someone who so thought quickly disabused of this fact.

Herein lies a valuable parallel experience for the life of stewardship: it is necessary to yield, to surrender, not to hold on to.
Freedom requires that we be unattached to persons and things so
that nothing threatens our choices and that our grasping does not
impede the growth process for things around us.

1 Samuel tells the story of Hannah, a woman who has been
barren and who yearns for a child. Her prayers are so poignant and
so intense that the temple rabbi wonders whether she has been
drinking (1 Sam. 1:14). But Hannah answered, "No, my lord, I am
a woman sorely troubled: I have drunk neither wine nor strong
drink, but I have been pouring out my soul before the Lord" (1
Sam. 1:15). Part of Hannah's prayer—and it is not an unusual
feature—is that if she gives birth she will not only encourage her
child's independence and growing away from her and her husband
but that she will formally surrender her child in his infancy to her
God. "And she vowed a vow and said, 'O Lord of hosts, if thou wilt
indeed look on the affliction of thy maidservant and remember me
. . . then I will give him to the Lord all the days of his life and no
razor shall touch his head.'"

Now there is no gift of God more precious, more mysterious
and more awesome than human life. And it is through this gift that
woman can instruct us: even this is a gift to be shared. To be a good
mother is to be a sharer.

In fact, we know a person to be "mother" by how she deals
with that which she could irresponsibly control but freely chooses
not to. 1 Kings 3 is illustrative. The story is Solomon's handling of a
difficult situation involving two women who claim mothership of
an infant. Solomon reveals that he knows something very fundamental about mothers: that is, that the real mother of the child

could not bear to see her child killed because her authority as
mother commands her to be responsible not only for giving life but
also for sustaining and perpetuating life. True to formula, the
mother of the living child in this story would rather see her child
given to someone else than to see it destroyed.

A good steward would behave in like fashion. Stewardship
demands a similar sentiment: utter sensitivity to living persons and
things and in the dignity that we confer on them. We honor these
things by not claiming them as our own, but by bequeathing them
for future generations.

III
JUSTICE: THE MOTIVATION FOR OUR BEHAVIOR

Justice is in the human order what righteousness of God is in
the divine order of things. Justice demands right order in relationships and in possessions.

I do not know why it is that women of the Old and New
Testaments are as concerned as they are with issues of justice—
though it is a fact that the most powerful and the most influential
women of both covenants (Deborah, Esther, Judith, Jael, Abigail,
etc.) *are* involved with this question. My inclination as both
woman and as theologian is to suggest that the unusual perception
that women evidence in this area has to do with their identification
with the oppressed and their radical faith in Yahweh that relied on
his doing what they were powerless to do. Women learned early in
Judaic history that to rely on any earthly power leads to temporal
solutions and that ultimate vindication and power comes only from
God.

Frankly, it comes increasingly less as a surprise to me to find
women in the Judaeo-Christian tradition as sensitized as they are
to issues of justice; their consciousness has been raised the hard
way.

One of the clearest justice statements of the New Testament is
made by a woman, and a singularly important woman, Mary.
Protestant theologians have recently taken to suggesting that Mary
should be reinvestigated and reinvigorated as a role model for

women. While my own sentiments support this type of endeavor, I am also led to suggest that Mary would not only provide an adequate role model for women, but for stewards as well, and most particularly with reference to the question of justice.

It is in Mary's prayer of the prophetic tradition placed on her lips in chapter 1 of the Gospel of Luke that she, like women of the Bible before and after her, maps out a liberative message of salvation promised by God to his people. In that message, Mary announces, in modern terminology, (1) a cultural revolution in which the proud are replaced by the poor and simple ("He has scattered the proud in the imagination of their hearts: and has exalted those of low degree"—Lk. 1:51-52); (2) a political revolution where the power passes from the mighty to the masses and where traditional political structures crumple; and (3) an economic revolution which provides, finally, food for the hungry and starving of the world while the rich "he has sent empty away." Mary, then, in that prophetic tradition enunciated by Hannah before her, proclaims a reversal of values: where the have's exchange places with the have-not's. It is not simply a case of the hungry being fed; it is more precisely and poignantly a situation where the hungry are fed and the fed are hungry. It has been observed that Mary has often been regarded as the comforter of the disturbed when she is far more accurately the disturber of the comfortable. Certainly, the socially radical statement that the Gospel writers chose to give her elevates her from accepting the status quo and urges us to consider a new model, and a feminine one at that, of stewardship.

CONCLUSION

Because of the burgeoning field of women's studies and the voluminous material that accrues each week, I have chosen in this outline to suggest only a few of the points of compatibility between the "feminine" and stewardship.

The very strong *a priori* that urges me to pursue this line of thinking emerges from a conviction that a complementary symbol system (male and female) is the most viable to sustain life because what it represents is the fullness of life. In concrete application of principles of stewardship, it is very frequently the male point of view that dominates. The preceding pages modestly offer the suggestion that the feminine dimension offers a healing balance and freshness to very real and human concerns of our brothers and sisters.

The Role of Property in an Economic System

Charles K. Wilber

Before we can talk about the role of property in an economic system we have to consider the purpose of an economic system. Basically it is a collection of social institutions and behavioral patterns that enable many people to work together to achieve goals that could not be so well attained individually.

Goals of an Economic System

There are many ways to classify goals, but the following, while not exhaustive, should enjoy widespread support among Christians and others who are concerned with the conditions of humankind in the modern world:

1. Overcoming scarcity both collectively and individually.
2. Generating and extending freedom of choice.
3. Fostering the conditions for right relations among people—fellowship.

Every society—past, present and future—has the task of organizing a system for producing and distributing the goods and services it needs for its own perpetuation. It must overcome scarcity by devising social institutions which will mobilize human energy for productive purposes. This productive effort must be enough to provide the total quantity of goods and services needed and must be allocated in such a way that the desired kinds of goods and services are produced. If any society is to maintain its ability to produce what it needs, it must distribute that production among its members in such a manner that they will have both the capacity (health and skills) and willingness (incentive) to continue working.

Feudalism, capitalism, and socialism all have had to devise social institutions to carry out these tasks. One of these key social institutions is the ownership system of productive property. Under capitalism a system of private property coupled with free exchange in markets has been relied upon to overcome scarcity. Under socialism a system of public property coupled with central planning has been relied upon. I will spell out the details later in the paper.

Our second goal—freedom of choice—has not been achieved by most societies in history. Freedom of choice means freedom to choose which consumer goods you want to buy, which occupation to pursue, which leader to help select and so on. In traditional societies freedom of choice was a moot point. Tradition determined occupation. Self-sufficiency and poverty meant that few consumer goods were purchased. Rulers were selected by tradition or force. Proponents of capitalism argue that its chief virtue is that not only is it productive but it maximizes freedom of choice. Proponents of socialism argue that meaningful freedom of choice requires worker control of production, minimum income levels for all, and a political mechanism to give us the kinds of communities and environments we want and need to survive.

Our third goal has never been achieved in the past and may never be fully achieved in the future, but it remains a goal to be sought after. The social institutions devised to ensure adequate production and to enable freedom of choice should also foster fellowship among the people of that society which will allow each to develop his/her potential. Fellowship thrives where people are led to cooperate in social endeavors and where there is time and opportunity to relate with each other as loving, sharing human beings. Fellowship is encouraged where there is a minimum of social forces that erect barriers among people. For example, extreme income inequality makes fellowship next to impossible. Emphasis on individual self-advancement makes fellowship and solidarity difficult to maintain. Race, class, and sex discrimination generate hostility which destroys the possibility of right relationships among people.

It needs to be noted at the outset that it may be difficult to reconcile the conflicting demands of three goals. Any set of social institutions will embody them in an imperfect way. Like freedom and order or justice and peace, they co-exist with a degree of tension even though it be a creative tension. Different peoples at different times will assign greater value to one of the goals over another. For example, proponents of capitalism place great value on overcoming scarcity and freedom of choice; in fact, they argue that the latter makes the former possible. Fellowship is seen either as a by-product of freedom of choice or, when pursued directly, in conflict with the first two goals. Many socialists, on the other hand, argue that fellowship fosters productivity and their interest in freedom of choice concentrates on its implementation in the workplace.

Role of Property in Achieving These Goals

As the traditions and legal restrictions of feudalism broke up at the end of the Middle Ages, they were replaced by an expanding system of private property where production was carried on for private profit and where those who did not own productive property sold their labor to those who did. Pursuit of self-interest was seen as the motive force of this new system that Marx called capitalism. Since an uncoerced person could be depended upon to act rationally to maximize his/her individual self-interest, it was thought possible to set up an automatic, self-regulating mechanism to manage economic affairs. These free choices were expected to overcome scarcity and result in the common good through the automatic adjustments of free exchange in markets. Thus one of our goals, freedom of choice, is seen also as a means to achieve the first goal of overcoming scarcity.

The first goal requires that society allocate its capital, labor and natural resources so that the needed (or desired) goods and services are produced and distributed in such a way that people are able and willing to go on producing.

From Adam Smith to today, mainstream economists have argued that the best way to overcome scarcity and to maximize personal freedom is to rely on the individual's pursuit of self-interest in a private property system regulated by the forces of market competition, where the government acts as the neutral umpire of the rules of the economic game. In order to maximize his/her income each person would have to produce something (product, service or labor) which others wanted and were willing to pay for. This, then, is the way to maximize production: to allow each person to produce whatever he/she can and to sell it on the market and attempt to gain the greatest income.

Since Adam Smith, economists have believed that the social institution of private ownership is necessary and beneficial if self-interest is to lead to society's economic welfare being maximized. This contrasts rather sharply with earlier thinking on the institution of private ownership. Medieval scholars had generally felt that private ownership of property was at best a concession to human weakness. The Catholic Church, then, as it still does today, practiced communal ownership in its convents and monasteries, but allowed the institution of private ownership to exist among the laity. In a truly sinless society of Christian brotherhood, communal ownership of property would be ideal. However, the Church conceded that human society was not sinless, and among such people common ownership would not lead to the common good. So common ownership was the rule for the holy orders, and private property was the rule for the secular population. This was a part of the medieval dual code of morality: a very strict code for religious and clerics and a less strict code for the laity.

John Locke argued that private property was a necessary part of a good society. Locke based his argument on a labor theory of property. Private ownership of property is justified by and derived from the labor of its owner. "The labor of man's body and the work of his hands we may say are properly his. Whatsoever then he removes out of the state that nature has provided and left it in, he hath mixed his labor with it, and joined to it something that is his own, and thereby makes it his property."[1]

This labor theory of property came to be one of the crucial elements of the classical economic doctrine. Because a person had wrested the soil from the state of nature and had cut the trees and so on, then that land should be his/hers and he/she should be entitled to use it for whatever purpose he/she saw fit, and so should his/her children and grandchildren. There was considerable debate on this subject throughout the seventeenth and eighteenth centuries. The English levelers and diggers at the time of the Cromwellian Revolution had insisted that large private fortunes were obtainable only by theft. They contended that no one person could produce a great fortune by his/her own individual efforts. Consequently, one person could acquire great wealth only by appropriating some of the wealth created by others. For example, the Standard Oil Company was built by the efforts of many thousands of people drilling, refining, and selling oil—and yet one man, Mr. John D. Rockefeller, ended up owning most of the Standard Oil Company. The levelers and the diggers would argue that this was only accomplished through appropriating the wealth produced by others.

It was left to Thomas Robert Malthus to present the modern case for private ownership of property. Malthus was a minister who had been repelled by the utopian idealism of the utilitarian philosophers of his time. He was appalled at the doctrine of the ultimate perfectibility of man. He was convinced that people were lazy, indolent, and slothful, and that they would not work unless forced to. There were only two forces that could make people work. One was the whip of hunger and poverty. The other force which would drive people to work was the chance of acquiring great property: "According to our past experience and the best observation which can be made on the motivations which operate on the human mind, there can be no well-founded hope of obtaining a large produce from the soil but under a system of private property. It seems perfectly visionary to suppose that any stimulus short of that which is excited in man by the desire of providing for himself and family and of bettering his condition of life should operate on the mass of society with sufficient force and constancy to overcome the natural indolence of mankind."[2]

What keeps a system of private property based on self-interest from degenerating into a jungle where the powerful oppress the weak? According to Smith and most mainstream economists since, competition is the great regulator of economic life. The forces of competition insure that the economy produces those goods which people desire in the quantities that are desired. Although Smith was not blind to the faults and machinations of businessmen, he argued that they could do little harm in a society dominated by freely competitive enterprise. If a businessman tried, for example, to sell his products at a higher price than the market price, he would lose all of his customers. No one would buy at a price above the market price. On the other hand, if he attempted to pay his workers less than the going wage, the workers would leave and go somewhere else where they could obtain the going wage. Therefore, the force of competition insured that workers were paid the going wage and consumers got their products at the lowest possible price.

As each individual attempted to maximize his/her income and become wealthy, he/she was thereby benefitting all society because society was made up of the individuals living in it. "As every individual, therefore, endeavors as much as he can both to employ his capital in the support of domestic industry, and so to direct that industry that its produce may be of the greatest value, every individual necessarily labors to render the annual revenue of the society as great as he can. He generally, indeed, neither intends to promote the public interest, nor knows how much he is promoting it." And next follows the most famous expression in all economic literature: "He intends only his own security; and by directing that industry in such a manner as its produce may be of the greatest value, he intends only his own gain, and he is in this, as in many other cases, led by an invisible hand to promote an end which was no part of his intention."[3] Thus, private profit and public welfare become reconciled through the impersonal forces of competition.

However, this private property system turned out to have an Achilles' heel: competition tended to destroy itself. Implicit in Smith's conception of competition is the analogy with centrifugal force—it just goes on and on. But competition turned out to be a foot race with the winner getting larger and larger and the losers dropping out of the race. As a result the U.S. economy today is characterized both by largeness of firms and by high concentration of firms in each industry.

To cite just a few examples: In 1973 General Motors, Exxon, AT&T, and Ford Motor Company each had net sales larger than the GNP of over 120 different countries. In 1968 the 200 largest manufacturing corporations held 60.9 percent of all manufacturing assets in the United States. More and more, industries are dominated by two to four firms. As a result, price competition has been replaced by competition in advertising and product differentiation.

Mainstream economists have split into three groups in response to these developments in the economy. Conservatives, led by Milton Friedman, argue that there is still plenty of competition in the economy and that the monopoly that does exist is caused by governmental interference with the workings of free markets.[4]

Anti-trusters, led by Willard Mueller, believe that the only solution is a vigorous policy of anti-trust enforcement. This will allow competitive forces in the economy to perform their regulative function.[5]

A third, somewhat heterogeneous, group of economists believe that economies-of-scale make large firms generally more efficient than small ones and thus competition must be supplemented with government regulation to control the outcome of private decision-making. These economists recommend policies ranging from greater disclosure of cost information to national economic planning accompanied by selective nationalization of firms.[6]

Human Behavior and Alternatives to the Present System

One thing unites economists, left to right, and that is the recognition that somehow resources—raw materials, capital, labor—must be allocated among competing uses. There are only three possible systems of allocation—markets, bureaucratic administration and altruistic sharing.

Most economists argue that since human behavior has a strong tendency toward self-interest, markets allow that self-interest to be channeled into productive purposes. Bureaucratic allocation raises several problems: massive amounts of information must somehow be made available to the central decision-making body; free choice must be surrendered, either democratically or dictatorially, to that same body; and the totalitarian tendencies resulting from uniting political and economic power in the same hands has to be dealt with.

Marxists, theologians of liberation, and radical socialists and anarchists of various hues have failed to deal with this fundamental insight when they talk about replacing production for profit with production for use.[7] It is not as easy as it sounds. The only radical alternative that has undergone the test of experience is the bureaucratic central planning of the Soviet Union and the Eastern European countries. Their record on our three goals is very mixed. They have made great strides toward the elimination of scarcity, particularly for the poorest, but free choice and fellowship are in little evidence and dictatorship and sycophancy are the rule.

In Cuba and China the regimes have tried to go beyond mere bureaucratic administration and create a "new man" who is cleansed from self-interest and is motivated by service to others. That is, altruistic sharing is the desired guide to allocation of resources. A job is chosen not for self-advancement but rather because it is of use to others. The results are not all in yet because the experience has been so short. However, the results so far are not reassuring. Again, while great achievements have been made in overcoming scarcity, the record is poor on free choice, except in the workplace, and ambiguous on fellowship.

The difficulties of using altruism to allocate resources are inherent in the idea. For me to allocate my time and income for others' welfare, I have to know what will increase other people's welfare. Not only is this amount of information impossible to obtain for more than a small group, but inevitably there will be conflicts between people's perceived interests. The only solution is a central body which somehow processes the information, establishes a priority list of needs, and informs me how they can be fulfilled. Again, however, the problem of centralized power rears its head. In addition, power of individual self-interest cannot be wished away as simply a manifestation of the class-nature of man which can be changed in the new society. Marxist historian Eugene Genovese recognized this problem when he wrote: "The nationalization of property and its attendant centralization of political power create powerful tendencies toward dictatorship and totalitarianism. Accordingly, they must be checked by the establishment of autonomous institutions—unions, newspapers, universities, etc.—with an adequate property base of their own. No faith can be placed in the supposed goodness of man; on the contrary, the essential doctrines of Christian theology and Freudian psychology concerning human frailty and potential aggression must be taken with deadly seriousness. To 'liberate' the good in people requires severe institutional and social restraints on what is and will remain the evil."[8]

Even in the most avowedly altrustically based society, the People's Republic of China, material incentives are used to overcome scarcity. While everyone wears Mao jackets, self-interest is accommodated by the fact that some are perpetually baggy and others hold an immaculate press. Party officials do not own but ride in limousines, and officers of the People's Liberation Army wear the same uniform as enlisted men except they have coat pockets—which is, of course, quite enough to establish differences between people. These relatively minor differences in rewards are supplemented by a pervasive system of command in the allocation of resources.

Experience yields only three ways to mobilize human effort for productive purposes: self-interest, command, altruism. Reliance on the acquisitive motive seems to contradict the major religious and ethical systems of the world. However, is a person moved by fear of the officials who command more admirable than one moved by self-interest? Reliance on altruism degenerates into reliance on fear because of its unworkability. However, even when this is all accounted for, it can be argued that the present extreme reliance on the acquisitive motive is unnecessary and probably harmful.

The existing income inequalities in most countries are unnecessary to mobilize human energy for production. Even with their incomes substantially reduced, business executives, college professors, physicians, and other high income earners would continue in their present work. They would still be rewarded well in monetary terms *and* in psychic income: pride, challenge, power, status, etc. Therefore, to overcome scarcity for the bottom twenty percent of the income earners and to provide them the means to exercise freedom of choice, we need to establish a minimum income guarantee, provide jobs for all who want to work, and finance the program by a radical redistribution of income.

The incentive of private ownership is still important for the ten million small businesses in the United States. However, for the five hundred largest corporations that produce seventy percent of all material output, the link between ownership and incentive has been greatly reduced if not severed. Executives now operate the businesses with minimum interference from owners. These corporations should be converted into cooperatives or nationalized. Ownership should be vested in the hands of townships, states, workers, or similar collective bodies. Communications firms should be owned by private individuals, churches, unions, and the like.

A central coordinating board would be necessary to ensure full employment, stable prices, and the implementation of social policy. Public policy would have to be developed in terms of growth vs. no-growth, public sector vs. private sector, and so on.

To keep these changes from degenerating into simply another form of centralized command, they would have to be instituted democratically. This, in turn, requires that a broad-based political party endorse and carry forward these and similar ideas. Ultimately, it must be the people who freely choose to restrict economic "liberties" in order that scarcity may be overcome for all, meaningful free choice will be extended to all, and the groundwork will be laid for the possible flowering of fellowship.

Fellowship: From Private Ownership to Stewardship

The changes called for above would sharply reduce the owner's absolute control over private property. Some of it should be nationalized, some taken over by cooperatives of workers, and so on. The guiding criterion should be stewardship. Individuals and collectives hold property and may use it as they see fit as long as the public interest is also served. Thus the acquisitive motive is not eliminated but rather muted and more carefully channeled for the public welfare. Competition should be supplemented by public control and ownership as the regulator of economic life.

So far I have discussed the first two goals of overcoming scarcity and preserving free choice. Little has been said about fellowship. Clearly a total reliance upon the acquisitive motive is inimical to the growth of fellowship. The public control measures advocated above must be supplemented with measures designed to allow fellowship to develop. There are many possibilities. Certainly an essential ingredient is the spread of worker self-management into the production sphere. Pride of workmanship and ideals of public service should be emphasized by the political parties, unions, churches, and collectives. Policies should be pursued that will regenerate neighborhoods and local communities.

These recommended changes will not come about overnight, but they are less improbable than the complete transformation of society and man envisioned by some Marxists and theologians of liberation. Also, these reforms should lead to a society far more humane than the existing one which is so tenaciously defended by conservatives. However, even if every reform were successful, our Christian belief tells us that sinful nature of man will still be there to ensure the continuation of the "human condition."

NOTES

1. John Locke, "Two Treatises of Government," *Great Political Thinkers,* ed. William Ebenstein (New York: Rinehart & Co., 1951), pp. 377-378.

2. Thomas Robert Malthus, "A Summary View of the Principle of Population," *Three Essays on Population* (New York: Mentor, 1960), pp. 33-34.

3. Adam Smith, *The Wealth of Nations* (New York: Modern Library, 1937), p. 423.

4. See Milton Friedman, *Capitalism and Freedom* (Chicago: University of Chicago Press, 1962).

5. Willard F. Mueller, "Antitrust in a Planned Economy," *Journal of Economic Issues,* Vol. IX, No. 2 (June 1975).

6. See Andrew Shonfield, *Modern Capitalism* (New York: Oxford University Press, 1965); Arthur Okun, *Equality and Efficiency* (Washington, D.C.: The Brookings Institution, 1975); John Kenneth Galbraith, *Economics and the Public Purpose* (Boston: Houghton-Mifflin, 1974).

7. See Assar Lindbeck, *The Political Economy of the New Left: An Outsider's View* (New York: Harper & Row, 1971).

8. Eugene Genovese, "What's the Most Important Thing You'd Like To See Happen in the United States in the Next Five Years?" *Mother Jones* (Sept/Oct., 1976).

Related Material for
Section I: Perspectives

Discussion Questions

1. Is God biased against the rich? (Sider)

2. Should the Church literally become a "poor Church" by giving away its vast wealth? (Sider)

3. Can the Church live a new model of economic simplicity and equality in radical discontinuity with the practice of surrounding society and still be an effective political witness in that larger society? If so, how? (Sider)

4. What has been your and your Church's understanding of stewardship? (Swartley)

5. What can we learn from the early Church Fathers? (Swartley)

6. Identify and discuss practical outcomes in your values and behavior when stewardship is related to (a) being God's image, (b) seeking justice in social and political relationships, (c) the needs of the hungry. (Swartley)

7. How does Jesus' love command relate to judgment on the basis of works? What is the relationship between salvation by faith and judgment by works? (Swartley)

8. What is the meaning of ethics? What is a value? An attitude? (Byron)

9. How would you describe the dominant values and attitudes in the United States toward the possession and use of material wealth? (Byron)

10. How do such attitudes affect persons in other parts of the world? (Byron)

11. What ethical issues should be of concern to participants in the economic system in the United States? (Byron)

12. In what ways does a feminine perspective enhance a discussion on stewardship? (Donnelly)

13. What does the notion of dignity imply? The notion of productivity? (Donnelly)

14. What does the notion of justice demand? (Donnelly)

15. What type of symbol system is most viable to sustain life? (Donnelly)

16. In what ways did Adam Smith's work represent a break with tradition? (Richards)

17. Discuss Milton Friedman's assertion that fundamentally there are only two ways to organize an economy. (Richards)

18. How can we get around the dilemma posed by the tendency of food aid to depress market prices and thereby discourage food production? (Richards)

19. Would it be easier to run American business on ethical principles if we had more international trade? Less international trade? (Richards)

20. How can the general public make it easier for businesses to adopt ethical policies in spite of the pressures of competition? (Richards)

21. What are the goals of an economic system? (Wilber)

22. What is the role of property in an economic system from a private ownership perspective? (Wilber)

23. What is the role of property in an economic system from a stewardship perspective? (Wilber)

Action Suggestions

1. Call together a group of people who share your concerns about stewardship. See if they would like to form an on-going worship/study/action fellowship. (Sider)

2. In this group, or with other friends, discuss the question: Are we asking government to legislate what we are not living in the Church? (Sider)

3. List five concrete steps your local congregation could take to express more fully the biblical teaching on economic relationships among God's people. (Sider)

4. To get in touch with what God intended in creation, block out a period of time in your schedule and meditate upon the meaning and purpose of the earth. (Swartley)

5. Reflect on the last six months. At what points did you follow the "love ethic" and give help to a neighbor in need? (Swartley)

6. Plan together as husband and wife which consumable items could be left off your shopping list. Calculate the amount of money that could be rechanneled for the needs of the hungry. (Swartley)

7. Use several recipes from Doris Longacre's *The More With Less Cookbook*. (See bibliography.) (Swartley)

8. Take your daily newspaper and rewrite five headlines in terms of an ethical question. (Byron)

9. Inquire around in your church, neighborhood, social or work communities and find out how people rank the right to private property among their personal priorities. (Byron)

10. List a "Bill of Obligations" for contemporary Americans. (Byron)

11. Rewrite the most recent Democratic and Republican Party platforms so that they could support without compromise a candidate named Jesus Christ. (Byron)

12. Begin a discussion group that will take some of the biblical selections mentioned in the article, investigate them from a critical point of view, and then use them as a starting point for discussion. (Donnelly)

13. Re-evaluate some of the ways you related to what you have. Decide if you need to change the way you do this in order to

better mirror what the author suggests in the meaning of productivity. (Donnelly)

14. Spend some time in a family discussion hearing each other talk about what motivates each person's behavior. (Donnelly)

15. Interview business leaders and labor leaders in your community concerning the objectives of the organizations they lead. Remember them in your prayers. (Richards)

16. Take several articles from your daily newspaper which discuss property questions and see whether they approach the issue from a private ownership perspective or a stewardship perspective. (Wilber)

17. The next time you gather with some of your friends, begin a discussion about how people use property. (Wilber)

18. Make a list of ways you can help spread worker self-management in your own profession and gradually begin to try to put these into effect. (Wilber)

Suggested Reading

Batey, Richard. *Jesus and the Poor: The Poverty Program of the First Christians*. New York: Harper's, 1972.

Byron, William J., S.J. *Toward Stewardship: An Interim Ethic of Poverty, Pollution and Power*. New York: Paulist, 1975.

"Economic Justice within Environmental Limits: The Need for a New Economic Ethic." *Church and Society*. New York: United Presbyterian Church, U.S.A., September-October 1976.

Finnerty, Adam. *No More Plastic Jesus*. Maryknoll, New York: Orbis Books, 1977.

Franz, Delton, Carl Kreider, and Andrew and Viola Shelley. *Let My People Choose: Christian Choice Regarding Poverty, Affluence, Standard of Living*. Scottdale, Pennsylvania: Herald Press, 1969 and Newton, Kansas: Faith and Life Press, 1969.

Harman, Willis. *An Incomplete Guide to the Future*. San Francisco: San Francisco Book Company, 1976.

Hengel, Martin. *Property and Riches in the Early Church*. Philadelphia: Fortress Press, 1974.

Heschel, Abraham J. *The Prophets*. New York and Evanston: Harper and Row, 1962.

Kauffman, Milo. *Stewards of God*. Scottdale, Pennsylvania and Kitchener, Ontario: Herald Press, 1975.

Laurentin, Rene, S.M. *Liberation, Development and Salvation*. Maryknoll, New York: Orbis Books, 1972.

Lodge, George C. *The New American Ideology*. New York: Knopf, 1975.

Longacre, Doris, Ed. *The More With Less Cookbook*. Scottdale, Pennsylvania: Herald Press, 1975.

Okun, Arthur. *Equality and Efficiency: The Big Trade Off*. Washington, D.C.: The Brookings Institution, 1975.

Sider, Ronald J. *Rich Christians in an Age of Hunger*. New York: Paulist Press and Downers Grove, Illinois: Intervarsity Press, 1977.

Simon, Arthur. *Bread for the World*. New York: Paulist Press, and Grand Rapids: Wm. B. Eerdmans, 1975.

Taylor, John V. *Enough Is Enough*. London: SCM Press, 1975.

Taylor, Richard K. *Economics and the Gospel*. Philadelphia: United Church Press, 1973.

Wallis, James. *Agenda for Biblical People*. New York: Harper, 1976.

II
Issues

Agriculture, Stewardship, and a Sustainable Future

Donald R. Geiger

A comparison of figures for world population growth and for world food production during the last several decades reveals that humankind is engaged in a race affecting the survival of many people. A recent conference on research imperatives related to crop productivity[1] focused on the prospect that the world's population almost certainly will double within the next few decades. Arguments about the exact date only distract us. The stark reality is that somehow the world needs to double its food production in a relatively short time span just to maintain the unsatisfactory status quo. To add to the challenge, this population growth will doubtless occur mostly in the less developed regions of the earth where food production is generally marginal and gains are hard-won. To have the people in these areas of population pressure depend heavily on imported food is not only technically impractical, but economically out of the question. Even if successful, the pattern would likely spawn prolonged economic dependence.

To make the situation even more difficult, a growing chorus of voices is warning us of pending environmental disaster brought on by humankind's efforts to utilize the earth's resources for its needs and desires. Conservationists and ecologically-oriented citizen groups are putting increasing pressures on industry and on others who are applying technology to develop the resources of the earth. In the area of agriculture, growing concern is being expressed over the use of fertilizers, herbicides, and insecticides, a course of action that threatens the very measures which have produced the most dramatic short-term gains in crop yield. Media coverage of actual cases of ecological disaster warns us that these concerns are not mere theoretical possibilities.

What are some answers to this development-conservation dilemma? One response is to disregard the cautions of those who see ecological disaster for humankind if we continue our present pattern of applying technology. The necessity to feed people is so basic that it seems almost unthinkable to constrain or curtail our efforts. In spite of risk it sometimes appears that we cannot afford the luxury of concern for the environment and the resulting constraints on interventions by humankind. Certain groups are fond of drawing scenarios which pit struggles for our very survival against the quest for an improved standard of living. Without entering into this debate, experience with the collapse of certain precariously situated ecosystems gives us an insight into the consequences when we disregard ecological balance.

Sahel: Victim of Misguided Development

Events in the Sahel region of Africa since the 1950's give us a dramatic example of short-term gains in agricultural productivity at the expense of long-term ecological stability.[2] Putting aside the motives and reasons for the development interventions, we see a rather clear pattern emerge. Programs promoting human health, veterinary care, and crop development, particularly in the early 1960's, brought an increase in resources to the Sahel. The result was an increase in the number of people and cattle and consequently increased exploitation of land prosperity. Distracted by short-term successes, decision makers seemed not to realize that the region was being moved steadily to the edge of ecological instability.

Although increased exploitation initially led to increased productivity, the argicultural ecosystem lacked the ability to sustain production in the long term. The relation between the people and their ecosystem was not sufficiently symbiotic to permit the system to survive the stress of periodic drought characteristic of the Sahel. Sparse and erratically-spaced rains worsened the malnutrition and even brought starvation to man and his cattle. The ecosystem, made unstable by overexploitation, degraded under the forces of wind and even of the rains that should have been a longed-for blessing.[3] This cycle, which ran its course in this fragile ecosystem during a rather short span, is not unlike the cycle which many environmental biologists see occurring more slowly even in developed countries because of present agricultural practices.

The answer to the dilemma posed earlier seems to be that we can ill afford not to be vitally and effectively concerned about the long-term ecological implications and the effects of humankind's quest for greater agricultural productivity. However there is a danger in uncritical commitment to ecological concerns. Some approach the population-food-survival dilemma with a single-minded focus on the disruptive aspects of humankind's attempts to harvest the earth. In its extreme form, the ideal proposed by these people is a return to undisturbed landscapes, fields, and forests. The price is a lowering of the earth's carrying capacity and an extremely curtailed standard of living. Consequently, imposition of this strategy is not likely to be supported or even tolerated by people in the world today. A stringent curtailment of efforts to develop natural resources is not a viable option today, nor does it appear necessary. A third option appears to be both possible and feasible.

A Symbiotic Approach

Rene Dubos, in an address to the 1976 Tyler Ecology Symposium, presented and developed the position that humankind can safely work at developing natural resources by setting up a symbiotic relationship with the ecosystem being developed.[4] By this symbiotic approach, a humanized ecosystem is maintained and people learn how to alter the earth profoundly without degrading it. By working in collaboration with nature, a humanized ecosystem is developed and maintained. Examples exist in some long-cultivated areas of the world where populations have lived in a productive and stable relationship with a drastically changed ecosystem. There are instances of agricultural production sustained over long periods of history though they may not be as productive, in the short term, as aggressively cultivated land. Without the input of people, these artificial ecosystems, including parks, gardens, forests, fields, and cities, would eventually return to wilderness. However, even their long past history of success does not guarantee a stable future unless the symbiosis is maintained and developed.

In order that people's attempts to create a productive human ecosystem be "safe," Dubos sees the necessity for certain attitudes and approaches which constitute a symbiotic relation between humankind and the ecosystem being transformed. The primitive-state model of managing human ecosystems relegates too passive a role to the human spirit and does not give sufficient credit to the ability of human wisdom to bring about the requisite symbiosis with the earth. At the opposite pole, there are those whose attitude is typified by the spirit expressed in the guidebook to the 1933 World's Fair celebrating the "Century of Progress"—"Science discovers, Industry applies, Man conforms." Implicit in this stance is a belief that the measure of progress is development, regardless of its consequences. Establishment of a symbiotic relationship and responsible stewardship cannot support actions carried out under this attitude.

The ethic of responsible stewardship, which is needed to promote this symbiosis, calls for a broad perspective and a long time frame for viewing the effects of human activities along with a greater sensitivity to the effects of relationships between humankind and the earth. The essentially Teilhardian view leads humankind to take responsibility for analyzing, planning, and carrying out its destiny. To establish the basis for the analysis, several basic questions need to be addressed.

1. What are the basic problems facing today's world with regard to its attempts to pursue agricultural development in both developing and more developed regions?

2. What are the guiding ideas in seeking a solution to these problems?

3. How can we convert the guiding ideas into a workable program?

Basic Problems

Looking at the development of our earth as it has been practiced by humankind, we see that there are a number of areas in which efforts are needed in keeping with responsible stewardship. People need wilderness areas relatively undisturbed by human intervention. These are places for production of certain natural resources, and, particularly, places for solitude and renewal of the human spirit. Communion with the rest of creation renews us, and so wilderness areas must be preserved and the impact of people minimized. In addition, humankind needs centers of dwellings and work which are not destructive of the human person.

To supply the needs for food, fiber, and other renewable resources a major part of our earth is dedicated to the practice of agriculture in its wide sense. Gardens, pastures, and farmlands are kept in a state of productivity by human skill, diligence, and management ability. In wilderness areas, as well as in the humanized ecosystems, conservation practices are needed as dictated by stewardship and the maintenance of a symbiotic relationship.[5] It is particularly this agricultural base that we will examine.

On a worldwide scale we are becoming aware of a phenomenon of degradation of ecosystems, particularly those which constitute our agricultural base. This process has been termed aridification.[6] Satellite-based ERTS and LANDSAT satellites give us a platform from which to take a global view of the earth's resources and enable us the better to study degradation of ecosystems. Analysis of the phenomenon has led to a number of conclusions:

1. Aridification is generally the result of certain practices of intensive agriculture, particularly as practiced during the past four decades. Basic causes of aridification include monoculture and certain forms of mechanization.

2. Characteristically it includes a change in the microclimate, that is, in the environmental conditions in the immediate vicinity of the crop plants. Related to this change are a decrease in the organic matter content of the soil, a decrease in vegetation cover of the land, and an increase in run-off of water and surface erosion.

3. Although the process of aridification is most quickly and dramatically seen in ecosystems which are fragile and easily disturbed, it is by no means limited to them. The U.S. dustbowl of the 1930's is a case in point of a fragile system which was rapidly degraded. However most U.S. agricultural lands show the same trend even if the results are not yet so devastating.

A specific example of aridification which has attracted attention in recent years is the process of desertification in the Sahel region of Africa.[7] Often ascribed to the failure of rains, the disaster was only triggered by drought. Overgrazing by cattle, sheep, and goats had denuded the soil of vegetative cover. Browsing by animals and collection of firewood had removed an excessive number of trees. Large tube-wells concentrated grazing by nomadic herds and led to the degeneration of large areas. As a result of removal of vegetative cover, erosion by wind and rain followed. Opening land for cropping and reduction of necessary fallow periods resulted from pressures for cash crops and the press of increasing population. We have here a dramatic example of the consequences of aggressive use of land resources for short-term returns.

The resulting situation worsens the microclimate, leads to erosion of soil and runoff of water, and lessens ground water recharge and soil water storage.[8] Some even believe that the massive changes of reflectance of solar radiation and heat transfer are producing undesirable changes in rainfall distribution. While the details of causal factors are debated, there is rather general agreement concerning the existence of desertification, its basic cause, and the importance of agricultural practices in bringing about degradation of the ecosystem.

Guiding Ideas in Working at the Problem.

To work at problems of the scope and complexity of aridification and desertification it is helpful to have a framework of guiding ideas that can provide a key to analysis.[9] One such basic concept is the need for successful systems to have the capability for being sustained over the long term.[10] A sustainable ecosystem is one which has sufficient balance between living systems and sufficient stability to allow the ecosystem to continue long-term existence in spite of occasional disturbances. The system must be structured and managed so that it has the potential for adaptation to these disturbances which are a normal part of the environment in question.

Another helpful point is the realization that we are dealing with a system which has social components as well as biological and agronomic ones. When we examine a social system such as that of the Sahelian countries or of the U.S. with a view to promoting its sustainability, it is helpful to be aware of the interactions taking place within it. There are exchanges of information, materials, and energy between the various components of the system. In society these major interactions follow discernible patterns. They are predictable because the interactions are directed toward certain relatively easily discovered ends. These interactions in various realms have become institutionalized. In our analysis we do well to consider the major realms of society:

1. The realm of *techno-economic structures*—here the interactions deal with economics and technology such as agriculture, industry, marketing and the like. The principles and practices of distributive justice constitute the ethical dimension.

2. The realm of *polity*—here the exchange deals with good management and organization. Social justice governs the organization with a view to the common good.

3. The realm of *culture*—this realm is made up of the values, myths, and mores of the society. Respect for cultural dimensions and freedom of their expression is the matter of cultural justice.

4. The realm of the *ecosystem*—this realm includes interactions between the plants, animals, people and their environment. The just use of resources respects and safeguards the interactions and balance between these elements. This ethical dimension is a major component of what may be called responsible stewardship.

These various realms interact within themselves and between themselves, sometimes in a constructive, balanced way and sometimes in degenerative cycles which lead to crises.

The population-food dilemma which we see in the Sahel is really a specific example of an exploitation-conservation dilemma facing U.S. agriculture as well. A major cause of the breakdown of a social system lies in structural contradictions or dilemmas such as this. Perhaps an example from our U.S. agricultural enterprise will illustrate the analysis in concrete terms. The data are largely from a study by David Pimentel and his associates at the New York State College of Agriculture and Life Sciences,[11] who recently analyzed the impact of land degradation in the U.S. on food resources. They note the favored agricultural status of the U.S. Only eleven percent of the earth's surface is considered arable and naturally suitable for cultivation, while in the United States twenty-five percent of the land is considered arable. But this belongs not only to us; we have a responsibility to our fellow humans as well as to future generations. The stewardship ethic extends our viewpoint in both space and time.

The question of national agricultural resource planning and management must deal with a structural contradiction that exists in U.S. society with regard to use of this resource. U.S. farmers, whose status is often precarious, have developed and institutionalized a pattern of decisions and actions which are directed toward a maximizing of production with a minimizing of expenditures to give the largest return with an acceptable risk. Decisions concerning the patterns of cropping, the types of tillage, and the amount of fertilizer, herbicide and pesticide applied are all aimed at this socially-accepted principle of action. Society in general and not just the agricultural sector is responsible for the principle and its basic short-sightedness. Another structured set of decisions and actions with implications for agriculture deals with the techno-economic realm. People demand convenient access to cities and markets, and this leads to use of land for highways, parking, and development. Still another set of structures, in the realm of ecosystems, promote efforts to orient land use in a way which will conserve our agricultural resources for the future.

Here we have cited at least three sets of institutionalized behavior patterns, working toward different goals, but with the common element of land use. This pattern has engendered a structural contradiction as a result of built-in conflicting demands placed on decision-makers and policy-makers dealing with land use. Will the land be used in a way to maximize profits, to maximize conservation in order to assure future availability, or to realize profit by sale to a developer?

A consideration of facts shows how decisions are structured in the U.S. in this area of agricultural land use. Each year more than 2.5 million acres of our 470 million acres of arable land are lost to urbanization and highways. Since 1945, the net loss was forty-five million acres or an area nearly the size of Nebraska. During the last two hundred years, at least one-third of the topsoil on U.S. farmland has been lost. Before 1940, nearly two hundred million acres had been lost to cultivation or seriously degraded for cultivation by erosion. And all of this has long-term consequences. Soil formation under normal agricultural practice is estimated at about 1.5 tons formed per acre each year. The average annual loss of topsoil from agricultural land is estimated at twelve tons per acre, eight times its rate of formation. Viewed from an ecosystem standpoint, soil erosion contributes to loss of arable land, silting of reservoirs, and degradation of rivers and lakes. The annual cost is estimated to be five hundred million dollars.

But these costs are to an anonymous "society," a faceless "them," while returns on the short term are more clearly seen as benefiting individuals. From an ecosystem viewpoint, it is wise to conserve soil, with a view to its future use as a resource. Contour plowing and crop rotation schemes and other available practices can reduce erosion to a level less than the rate of topsoil formation. But these land-management practices increase costs in time and fuel, costs borne by individuals, now. In practical terms, use of land according to the dictates of conservation is not being carried out extensively for a number of reasons. Pimentel and his associates[12] cite several of these related to structural contradictions, including the farmers' need for immediate income, the failure to appreciate the need for the recommended practices because of inertia and custom, and the existence of a large number of rented or corporate farms whose operators place short-range return over long-term soil quality. The cost of soil erosion represents a virtually insignificant loss per year while the cost of control is more apparent. Based on an investigation of corn growers in northeastern Illinois, it would cost about thirty-nine dollars per acre over a twenty-year period to practice soil conservation. Considering this cost and the increased return to the individual using soil conservation practices, the farmers actually would lose income by keeping soil losses below three tons per acre per year. But it would seem that future generations deserve this investment in their well-being. The just use of natural resources makes demands both with respect to space and time.

The alternative of return to an unmanaged, primitive ecosystem can be rejected out of hand. Then how can we safely pursue agriculture in the face of this structural contradiction between exploitation and conservation goals? In practice social justice and responsible stewardship demand that society and individuals expand their perspective to include the common good and future good of humankind. There are people in generations to come who will depend on inheriting a sustainable agricultural system. The U.S. has been graced with a disproportionate amount of arable land. In grateful response we need to look upon our resources as not just our own but to see them in relation to the millions who need a source of food available for trade or as relief in time of crisis. A national effort to insert the ethic of stewardship into agricultural planning is an important first step. Also, the goal of system sustainability needs to become a part of the value system of the various realms of society, particularly in regard to agriculture systems. Sustainability of the system is clearly related to the symbiotic relationship between humankind and the earth, supported by Dubos. The ability of the system to survive in the long term is promoted by converting contradictory social structures, such as those relating to agricultural land use, into "symbiotic" structures. Planning and decision-making for agricultural development need to incorporate the viewpoints of the various realms and the elements of justice related to each.

Tools for policy planning and analysis which enable one to see better the effects of contemplated actions have been devised.[13] These methods permit decision-makers to take into consideration the various realms and interests and relate these to the concerns of social, ecological and cultural justice. Decisions, such as those faced by persons responsible for agricultural planning, need to take into account these somewhat less tangible elements along with the more quantitative technical and economic factors. With the selection of appropriate methods and policies it should be possible to set up an agricultural system which favors ecosystem stability and sustainability. By adding societal dimensions, we should be able to have productive agriculture which can be managed on a sustained yield basis without deterioration of the agricultural resource base—a symbiotic relationship between the agriculturalists and their earth.

NOTES

1. A. Brown, T. Byerly, M. Gibbs and A. SanPietro, 1956, *Crop Productivity-Research Imperatives* (Michigan State University and C.F. Kettering Foundation, 1975).

2. N. Wade, "Sahelian Drought: No Victory for Western Aid," *Science* 185 (1974) 234-237.

3. N. MacLeod, "Food Production in Deserts," *Earth Resources Development Research Institute* (Washington, D.C., 1975).

4. R. Dubos, "Symbiosis Between the Earth and Humankind," *Science* 193 (1976) 459-462.

5. W.H. Thomas, Jr., *Man's Role in Changing the Face of the Earth*, Volumes I and II (University of Chicago Press, (1956) pp. 448 and 1193.

6. MacLeod, *ibid.*

7. Wade, *ibid.*

8. E. Zamierowski, D. Hornbach, and R. Fitz, Ecological Components of Climax Agriculture: An Example of Structuring Complex Feedback Systems, *International Conference on Cybernetics and Society. IEEE* (November 1976).

9. R. Fitz, Organizing for Development Planning: Methodology, Models, and Communication, *International Conference on Cybernetics and Society, IEEE* (November 1976).

10. D. Geiger and R. Fitz, Structural Modeling and Normative Planning for Ecosystems, *International Conference on Cybernetics and Society, IEEE* (November 1976).

11. D. Pimentel, D. Terhune, R. Dyson-Hudson, S. Rochereau, R. Samis, E. Smith, D. Denman, D. Reifschneider and M. Shepardd, "Land Degradation: Effects on Food and Energy Resources," *Science* 194 (1976) 149-155.

12. *Ibid.*

13. Fitz, *ibid.*

Stewardship and the New International Economic Order (NIEO)

Philip Land

For the poor nations, food and other agricultural production are linked inevitably with trade, financing of development and debt. There are two reasons for this. First, in the short run, at least, many poor countries will have to import some or most of their food. In the longer run most will have to produce their own food and other agricultural products. And while they ought to be reducing their reliance on foreign purchases of inputs for this—seed, fertilizers, pesticides, machinery, energy—there will always be some need for such buying. These short-run and long-run acquisitions will in the main have to be paid for. The second reason ties in with the first: agricultural development is both cause and effect of general economic development, and the latter is conditioned by trade, financing and debt.

What is the link of all this to the new international economic order? It is this: the old order enmeshed the poor countries in a power play that produced only enduring powerlessness, inequality and inability to develop. This essay first inquires into the roots of this inequity. Then, keeping in mind the poor countries' need to buy agricultural inputs and food, it examines some planks they want in a new international economic order.

But first a word about terminology. The rich countries lie mainly around the North Atlantic. It is now customary to refer to them as the north. The poor countries lie for the most part in the southern hemisphere and in Asia. These are commonly called the south. They are also called the third world (the second is the USSR together with the socialist states of Eastern Europe). The fourth world is a term now applied to the poorest segment of the third world. The third world embraces the oil-producers and certain other "middle income" countries enjoying annual growth rates of four percent per head—Mexico, Brazil, Argentina, Singapore, South Korea, etc.

There exists a wide gap between the north and south, with the exception in the latter of the wealthiest of the OPEC group. Up to now, that gap has been looked at in terms of the need to catch up. Now, more enlightened spokespersons of the south view the gap as a measure of the obstacles to their own, indigenous development, one that does not require "catching up." In short, it is a gap of domination and exploitation and opportunity denied.

The World Bank's president, Robert McNamara, in his October 1976 report to the bank's governors, gives these figures. Income per head in the north is running at $5,500, with even the best of the south (a few OPEC excepted) running far behind. Still, as pointed out above, the "middle income" countries are able to emerge from poverty, though the bottom forty percent haven't seen much of that potential for escaping poverty trickle down to them. Later we shall see that even the "middle income" nations encounter obstacles to their further progress.

Meanwhile the poorest countries, those averaging under $150 per person in 1975 and comprising over 1.2 billions, have to content themselves with annual increases of a bare two dollars a head. At the lower end of the spectrum of poverty this means further declines from already abysmally low levels of nutrition, and substandard housing and health. Three-quarters of a billion, says McNamara, live at the very margin of existence.

The North/South Gap

At the heart of this gap and underlying inequality of opportunity lies international order—or, in the eyes of the third world, international disorder. This results in a distribution of gains from international investment, trade, and technology that unduly favors the already rich and powerful nations. It is also locked in irremovability so long as decision-making in world bodies like the

International Monetary Fund remains the virtually exclusive privilege of the powerful rich. Practically speaking, these control credit movement around the world. This is a reflection of the same control of credit within the wealthy nations themselves where the poor get credit, if at all, on terms far less favorable than the terms enjoyed by the rich.

In the address referred to above, McNamara maintains that even though the debt of the poor nations is a great obstacle to their development, inaccessibility of credit is still more of a problem. What he has in mind is this. A few financial powers like the USA can finance their own deficits by creating their own short-term credit. In addition they have unlimited access to international credit. The weaker of the industrial nations of the north can get help on deficits from the IMF's Special Drawing Rights which are a paper credit created by the Fund. These are also available to the south but on very limited quotas. These quotas will not change easily, given the slight power the south has on IMF decision-making. Mahbub ul Haq, director of policy planning for the World Bank, estimates that of $130 billions of international reserves only about four percent goes to poor countries.

Who Gets Credit?

Credit is one form of purchasing power, and just as the rich within a nation who possess credit can move the market and thus production in accordance with their desires, so, at the world level, the rich nations with easy access to credit are in the driver's seat in world production. In the south the poorest nations are considered un-credit worthy. But even the "middle income" countries can't get credit on the same terms as countries in the north.

This view requires some qualification, for, as we shall see later, the south does receive credit from northern governments (but not much), the IMF and World Bank, and recently private banks. The terms on which they receive much of their credit appear excessively onerous to the south. In any case it is inadequate to their needs. Here they point out that governments of the north, in order to prevent those of its citizens with purchasing power from garnering too much of the nation's goods and services, redistribute income and credit to the poorer. Why, asks the third world, isn't there some such authority for fairer distribution of credit at the world level?

Inequity in World Trade

Another component of inequality is the international trading system. The south believes that the international trade system benefits the north disproportionately. Trade theory as expounded in the north would have it that the poor nations gain through trade from the rising prosperity of the rich. As the latter grow in industrial prosperity they require more raw materials. This causes prices of these to rise, thus benefiting the developing nations. Also, as labor costs rise in the industrialized world, investors shift their investment to the developing nations where labor costs are lower. This investment launches the poor world into industrialization. Also, in free exchanges the third world is at liberty to move labor as well as its capital into the industrial north.

Such freedom of labor to migrate is of course limited practically to cases of labor shortage, doctors and nurses. Unskilled labor migrates from south to north in Europe—but temporarily. Labor is returned home when depression hits the common market. Meanwhile, the north's capital tends to go where capital already is. U.S. investments are found overwhelmingly in Europe.[1]

If the flow of factors of production—labor and capital—bears little resemblance to that posited by trade theory, the same in the view of the third world can be said of the flow of raw materials and manufactured goods. The north is able to keep out of its markets competitive products. The north as a whole pours some $20 billions into protecting its farmers from the south's agricultural products. Industrial workers and investors are also protected.[2]

On one point of trade there can probably be little disagreement. This is that the value added to raw materials in the process of transformation go mainly to the rich industrial north. Haq argues that the annual bill paid by consumers in the north for beverages, foods and manufactured goods originating in the raw materials produced by the south amounts to over $200 billions. Of that, the primary producers get only $30 billions. Haq says that just as within a nation the farmer gets relatively little of the consumer's dollar, with most going to middlemen and distributors, the same is true in the case of the developing countries. The value added to the product of their fields goes in part to their own middlemen. But largely it goes to those who control most of the processing of these raw materials, the finishing of them and even their distribution within the developing world itself. And these are the processors of the rich world. Think of the big names in cocoa production.

If the rich industrial world could be persuaded to transfer to the south more of this processing and distribution of the south's own raw materials, the developing world would stand, according to Haq, to gain an annual $150 billions in earnings. If this be contrasted with the meager $8 billions of aid received from the twenty nations of the north's OECD, it is easy to see where the south's main reliance ought to be placed.

The UN's New International Economic Order

By now everyone knows that the new international economic order (NIEO) is the product of a series of UN meetings held at various levels and times but culminating in two special sessions of the UN, the sixth in April 1974 and the seventh in September 1975.

At first the north, especially the USA and West Germany, took fright at what they thought would emerge as a revolutionary threat to the world of free enterprise. Actually, far from being revolutionary, the NIEO is not even at all that new. Most of its proposals had already figured in the agenda of the First and Second Development Decade strategies of the UN.

What then is new? Really only these three focuses. First, surer control by the third world of its own resources. Second, a shift from emphasis on aid and other transfer of financial resources from north to south in favor of centering attention on a new deal in world economic power. Third is the already-mentioned lessening of concern for "closing the gap," with more emphasis on equality of opportunity for the poor nations so that they can make their way according to their own ideas and in self-reliance.

Equality of opportunity: this is the heart of the matter. To redress the existing imbalance of economic power[3] in the world and thus to advance equality of opportunity the NIEO proposes the following:

1. The regaining of full sovereignty and control of their national resources, including litoral and territorial waters. Two hundred miles is the figure the world is moving toward.

2. Gaining from their resources a livelihood and national development.

This latter implies freer entry for their products into the north and more remunerative prices for them.

We Want To Sell

On the first—freer entry—we have already alluded to the power of the industrial north to exclude from their markets. The common market countries (with the exception of West Germany) have shown themselves much more disposed than the USA to open their shores to raw materials and light manufactures from the third world. The USA remains excessively protectionist. It should be recognized that what the south asks is only what the north professes to believe in—free markets. (A more exhaustive account of the 77's demands would include their desire to share such lucrative appendages to trade as shipping, insurance and market distribution of products.)

And For Better Prices

On the second—more remunerative prices—the south wants prices that will assure a better and more stable income. This requires price agreements, a major focus of all UNCTAD meetings. At the fourth, in Nairobi, in May 1976, the south got the agreement—a highly reserved and, on the part of the USA, reluctant one—to initiate before the end of 1976 preparatory meetings in anticipation of price negotiations on twenty raw materials to be begun early in 1977. The agreement embraces the creation of buffer stocks required for price stabilization and the financing of such. A single fund for all twenty commodities is proposed with West European support. The USA remains adamantly opposed to a common fund.

It is the view of the USA, together with West Germany, with Japan and Great Britain in weaker support, that commodity agreements are the wrong road for the south to go. They argue, first, that such agreements are hard to negotiate and police—and indeed experience fully supports this. In addition, they maintain that benefits of such would go to countries already well-off like North America and the USSR which are important producers of raw materials. At the same time a rise in price of raw materials would be a blow to poor countries importing these. UNCTAD's secretariat believes that differential treatment could avoid undue gains by the north while injury to the poor nations of the south could be remedied by grants.[4]

Pending such agreements, and, in any case, for those products for which price arrangements prove more difficult, the third world seeks compensatory payments against shortfalls in export earnings.

What can be said in summary about chances for such price negotiations? Stabilization in itself could be managed by the 77 without assistance from their industrial buyers. It would be enough to regulate market supply with the aid of buffers created by themselves. But stabilization of prices at more remunerative prices runs against the resistance of the north to higher prices. The south has little control over the industrial users. These will resist too high a price and look for substitutes. Witness the present incipient coffee rebellion.

Let Us Grind Your Coffee

Earlier on we saw how lucrative is the processing of raw materials. Of the $200 billions the consumer pays for the final product the producers of the original raw materials receive only some $30 billions. Understandably a third plank of the NIEO is a fairer sharing in processing. This could result in lifting income of the south as high as $100 billions, far beyond what they can even hope to receive in aid.

A fourth plank in the NIEO responds to the south's fear that continuing inflation in the industrial world can wipe out gains from sale of raw materials as well as eventual processing and export of manufactured goods. Of the current huge deficits burdening the third world's non-oil producers, only one-third is owing to the hike in oil prices. The other two-thirds is accounted for by rises in prices of the north's industrial goods.

In order to keep prices of the raw materials they sell in pace with the chronically inflationary prices of the industrial goods they must buy, the south proposed indexation of prices. The USA and West Germany pose problems with indexation, and there are such. But if we think them insuperable, it is surely our responsibility to propose alternatives since we are responsible for the south's loss of purchasing power.

Up to Our Necks in Debt

The fifth and final plank of the NIEO to be considered responds to third world debt, a total of some $180 billions. Deficit on current account is running right now at $50 billions. This is a huge jump over 1974 and reflects up to one-third the hike in oil prices and the other two-thirds the chronic inflation in the industrial world. To meet amortization and interest on the debt the third world will in 1977 have to come up with $20 billions.

Who owns the debts? Governments own some. The International Monetary Fund and World Bank own some. Private banks own a surprisingly high share.

To meet their obligations the south makes several proposals in the NIEO. First they want an international central bank to replace national banks as a future source of development financing. To this bank would be accorded jurisdiction over the creation and control of international reserves. These in turn would replace national reserves of dollars, marks and gold in international payments. These reserves would expand to meet the needs, not just of the

North Atlantic as is true presently, but of all nations, including the developing ones.

For longer-term development capital—the poor countries meet about eighty percent of their needs from their own resources—the south makes several proposals.

First, they return to insist on the public aid target of 0.7 percent of the gross national product set by the UN for the Second Development Decade. This is a target that the USA rejects. As public aid, the 0.7 percent ought, the NIEO insists, to be given on a purely concessional basis.

Next, the third world asks that the IMF's SDRs (special drawing rights)—costless figures on a ledger—be linked to third world development. To the contention that SDR's were created, not to support development, but a liquidity required for world trade, the developing countries make this answer. Turn them over to us (you lose nothing since they are costless) and we will quickly put them into circulation in the industrial world as we use them up to purchase the equipment we need for our development. So used, they would constitute a second Marshall Plan. There is possible conflict between the goals of liquidity and development, into which we cannot enter here.

Finally they call for sales of IMF gold in addition to the first, already effected through the Fund's 1975 agreement at Kingston, Jamaica.

There are also several long-term financing requests made upon the World Bank in addition to the various forms of short-term credit already furnished by the bank, but (in the eyes of the third world) in insufficient amounts. Space does not permit consideration of these.

What's Wrong with a World Tax?

To assure funding of these, the south in the seventh special session made still another request. This is for a degree of automaticity. Their problem here is that even where the north is inclined to some generosity, ardor quickly cools when the north feels a financial pinch, as at present. How to do this? Many proposals have been made—tax use of seabeds, one or other non-renewable resource, pollution of waters, arms sales. The linking of SDR's might be considered such a tax. An automatic transfer of funds would, the south recognized, constitute in effect a tax on the rich countries. Since the rich will not be inclined to tax themselves in any such ways, UNCTAD has proposed that the north accept a tax imposed antecedently by the south. This might take the form of one or a few cents tacked onto the sale price of commodities exported to the north like coffee, cocoa, and copper. Such antecedent taxing can of course be imposed only by those poor countries possessing a salable surplus.

The developed countries object that such taxation would in no way benefit them. But this objection rests upon a possible myopic view, for transfer of income from rich to poor can, by elevating the condition of the weaker members, contribute to the common welfare at the world level just as it can at the level of a single nation.

And So to Stewardship

To round out this chapter we have to say a word about stewardship and the NIEO. Since other chapters dwell on scriptural and theological foundations of stewardship, it will suffice here to link stewardship to trade, aid, debt and development in general.

Recipients of God's immeasurable bounty, we give it back to him and so praise and worship him by sharing this bounty with others.

Specifically, we exercise stewardship over the world's resources by a sharing, caring, sparing use of them. Ultimately, husbandry begins with needs. We use God's gifts to respond to human and social needs, with priorities established in favor of the necessities of food, clothing, shelter, health, education and work for all in accord with the exigencies of each people's culture. Only after these are satisfied should response be made to the desires of the more affluent.

Stewardship will mean that the nations shift from production for profit to production for need. Obviously, a needs-oriented economy will not be achieved where incentive to produce is lacking. What has to be worked out is legitimate profit for entrepreneurs.

But even more important is incentive for the little people who make up the billions of the poor world. Such incentive does not exist where they are deprived of a chance for land ownership or job tenure or where governments siphon off most benefits and services to the rich, land owners, and the military.

Stewardship calls upon the richer nations to share more fairly with the poorer. We are our brother's keeper. We are called to live in solidarity because all of us are born into the family of humankind before being born into the fellowship of any particular nation.

This call to solidarity receives another expression as an obligation of international social justice. If the peoples of the world constitute a oneness, then they have some things they hold and share in common, call it a common good or "commons." If there is such a common good, then there must be an obligation in justice to achieve this. Such obligation at the national level we call social justice. It becomes international social justice if it is to be achieved at the world level.

Specifically we share (in interdependence) the limited—at least relatively limited—resources of our planet. We must be mindful that they were destined by the Creator for the service of all humankind.

We therefore share, as one people, common needs, and we meet these by sharing the world's "commons" of land, water and air.

Challenge to our living up to this sharing of resources (and they are intellectual and cultural as well as material) comes at several points of our chapter. Suffice it to mention them.

The rich and powerful cannot deny reasonable access to any resources held in superabundance. "Feed the man dying of hunger," said the fathers of the early Church, "otherwise you have killed him." The right to food, elsewhere in this volume substantiated, has here its implications. First is the right to emigrate in search of food and employment. Second is the right to access to the human patrimony of intellectual achievement, industrial arts and technology—and this on reasonable terms. Third is the right to access to markets and to be able to sell one's product there at remunerative prices. This is part and parcel with the right to support oneself which is implicit in the right to life. True, all these rights must be dovetailed with the rights of others to control migration and to avoid injury by access to technology or markets.

NOTES

1. Two other factors presently limit availability of capital. First is stringency experienced in the industrial world at least for some types of long-range investment, e.g., on energy. Second is the unwillingness of many northern investors to invest in the south, especially Latin America, given the latter's sensitivity to foreign investment. The north demands "an atmosphere favorable to investment." The south requires that the northern investor respect more the right of the poor to control their own resources and to share more fairly the profit of enterprise conducted in their territory.

2. Arguments grow heated when we try to figure out just how much protection is justified. Many American labor unions are vociferous in demanding exclusion of goods that threaten their jobs. With unemployment running at eight percent, this is highly understandable. And not until governments will have worked out satisfactory adjustments for displaced workers can we expect these to be very concerned about the plight of the poor world.

3. Other sources of inequality of opportunity than those mentioned in the text are, first, multinationals; secondly, decision-making within the IMF and the World Bank group. On the former the South wants to change the terms of leasing and contracting, reduce the concessions made earlier in favor of the MNCs, get a fairer sharing of profits, force the MNCs to put more of their own resources into the enterprise rather than draw so much from the poor host country. On decision-making they want change in power structures to afford them more voice.

4. An alternative route to higher prices got much attention at the Sixth Special Session but less at the Seventh. This is the creation of mini-OPECs for copper, bauxite, manganese, and the like. The Third World fondly dreams of imitating the extraordinary success of the oil-producers. But two factors work against almost all other raw materials. First, world demand for these is nowhere as great. Secondly, substitutes are generally available and profitable to introduce when prices for raw materials rise high enough.

Concentrated Ownership of Land

Mary Margaret Pignone, S.N.D.

In October 1957 the Soviet Union placed its first satellite, Sputnik I, into orbit. As a child of thirteen who literally "felt" that satellite orbiting overhead, I wondered about the possibility of human beings ever walking on the moon. That prospect had been moved from the pages of science fiction to the headline news. The question then struck me: Who would own the moon? On clear fall nights as I looked at the great expanse of black sky the idea of someone or some country actually owning the moon impressed me as being utterly absurd. The more I thought about it, the more convinced I became that if it was absurd to think of a privately owned moon, it was just as absurd to think of a privately owned earth.

Now, some years later, the question of ownership of the earth is again paramount in my thinking. More than the concept itself, the results of concentrated, unrestricted ownership strike me not only as absurd but also as wrong. There are two main concerns: stewardship of the land itself as a precious, irreplaceable, absolutely indispensable resource, and hunger in the world as a problem of concentrated ownership.

This chapter is about land in the United States and what is happening to it. The purposes of the chapter are: (1) to demonstrate the increasing concentration of land ownership and the relationship between control of land and capital and the problem of hunger in the world; (2) to describe the destruction of the land which accompanies huge corporate ownership; (3) to outline what national polices encourage concentrated land ownership and ignore constant abuses; (4) to offer some alternatives and to recommend needed policy changes; and (5) to argue why and how this approach should be considered in moral terms.

112

I

CONCENTRATED OWNERSHIP OF LAND

The fact that land reform is not the number one item on the domestic U.S. agenda is a tribute to the corporate public relations industry and an indictment of educational institutions, the communications media, and the institutional Church. The problem of hunger in the world cannot be solved until the questions of ownership and use of land are recognized as problematic.

There are several false myths about land use in the United States that contribute to an incorrect formulation of national questions. The first myth states that we are a society of small land holders and that land reform is only a concern for foreign, principally Latin American countries. A society of small land holders was indeed Jefferson's ideal. But this dream has gone largely unrealized.

Today, one-third of the nation's land is still owned publicly, mostly by the federal government. Of the two-thirds in private hands it is estimated that as much as *sixty-five percent is owned or controlled by only five percent of the nation's population.* [1]

This paper will focus on two concentrations of land ownership. The first concentration is the growing consortia of energy, timber and railroad conglomerates. The second concentration of land is solidifying in the agricultural sector. There, huge corporations are developing monopoly control of the food industry. In too many cases, these two powerful spheres of concentrated corporate ownership overlap.

Energy, timber and railroad industries own enormous tracts in the U.S. There is no immediate way of knowing how much of the country is controlled by this powerful group. We have no national figures on land ownership. Some picture of the ownership pattern, however, can be patched together.

A study published by the Center for Rural Studies in 1972 found that the top twelve timber companies controlled close to forty million acres of land in the United States, eight of the top fifteen oil companies controlled almost sixty-five million acres, and only four western railroads owned nearly twenty-seven million acres. These companies are about half the major energy, timber and railroad corporations in the U.S. today. Were land ownership data available for all corporations these figures would be substantially increased, perhaps doubled.[2]

In some instances entire states are owned and/or controlled by the energy-timber-railroad network. In December 1974, Tom Miller, an investigative reporter for the Huntington *Herald-Dispatch*, revealed that of the fifty-five counties in West Virginia, twenty-seven had over half their land owned by corporate out-of-state interests. The top ten owners were either mineral, timber or railroad companies.[3] A dozen pulp and timber companies own an estimated fifty percent of the state of Maine while other absentee ownership in that state controls an additional thirty percent of the land area.[4] A single company, Burlington Northern Railroad, owns one-tenth of the state of Montana.[5]

Less than fifty energy, timber and railroad companies, as noted above, own an estimated one-fifth of the nation's non-public land. They also lease a great deal of the publicly held land. It can be argued that since stockholders are the real owners, the concentration is not nearly so great. Ownership of corporate stock, however, is also very concentrated. As few as two percent of all U.S. taxpayers receive over three-quarters of all dividends and capital gains in the United States.[6] That concentration is magnified by the number of interlocking directorates in major corporations. The Center for Science in the Public Interest found no less than 460 interlocking directorates and advisory committee connections in the eighteen largest oil companies. Links were with other energy companies, with banks, insurance companies and educational institutions.[7]

More alarming still is the realization that most currently used sources of energy (i.e., non-renewable fossil fuels) are controlled by the same giant conglomerates. Of the top fifteen coal producers in this country eight are actually oil companies, and the top twenty gas producers are *all* oil companies. In fact, oil companies own sixty percent of all natural gas reserves. Oil is also moving into uranium and geothermal steam. Some forty-five percent of known uranium reserves are controlled by oil.[8]

Couple this with the fact that much of the government-owned energy reserves are leased by these same companies, with the fact that excessive cash flows within the energy industries and a favorable tax structure encourages heavy investment in agricultural land, plus the fact that in the past thirty years farming has been turning into a highly mechanized, energy-dependent industry, and the dimensions of this concentration of land ownership become staggering.

The second concentration of land ownership that is increasingly alarming is the rapid monopolization of agriculture. In terms of corporate assets, twenty-five of the thirty largest corporations in America are engaged in agriculture. Included in that number are nineteen oil, gas, and chemical companies.[9] Of even more concern is a 1973 congressional study that found that a majority of those corporations are controlled by only eight institutions, including six banks.[10]

Over sixty percent of the best farmland in Iowa and Illinois, states generally associated with family farm agriculture, is rented, suggesting a high degree of absentee ownership. Six midwestern states, Iowa, Kansas, Minnesota, Missouri, Nebraska and South Dakota, through recent legislation, require corporations engaged in farming to file special reports. As many as 9,000 reports have been filed in the six states at present, and strong evidence indicates that a number of corporations are failing to file. This number of corporate farms is three times greater than a 1969 Department of Agriculture study estimated. Even if seventy-five percent of these corporate farms are family corporations, the growth of non-family corporations engaged in agriculture is still startling.[11] Five and a half percent of our "farmers" control over half of our farming land. Companies such as Standard Oil, Getty, Gulf and Western, Penn Central, and Tenneco are now into agriculture.[12]

The decline in family ownership of farms is noticeable also in the south where the drop in black ownership is particularly significant. In 1910 blacks were operating 890,000 farms with full or partial ownership of about fifteen million acres. Black ownership today is down to almost five million acres, a drop of over sixty-six percent. Approximately 300,000 acres of land is lost to black ownership annually. If that trend continues, the remaining blacks in the rural south will be landless before the end of the century.[13]

It is likely that the decline in black ownership reflects the decline in small farm ownership that is characteristic of the country as a whole. A December 1976 USDA Statistical Reporting Service release shows that the number of farms in the nation has declined about 479,000 over the past ten years, or almost 1,000 farms per week. Some of this land is simply being removed from agricultural use entirely. Every year, according to a recent U.S. Soil Conservation Service estimate, two million acres of agricultural land is lost to urban sprawl, highways, airports and other such uses. However, while the number of farms in the U.S. has declined by fifteen percent in the last ten years, the amount of land in farming has only declined by four percent in the same period. Clearly there is a strong trend toward fewer and bigger—not farms, but rather, agricultural industries.

What relationship does this have with world hunger? The situation in which we are finding ourselves is one where the production of our food is dependent upon those who control capital. This gives competitive advantage to those who can obtain capital at lower interest rates. Big corporations are thus able to earn greater profits more easily than independent family farmers.

What and how much should be produced and how it will be sold are questions that will be answered on the basis of what guarantees the greatest return on investments. Ability to pay, not human need, is the dominating principle in this food system. Were income distributed worldwide and evenly, this sytem would present fewer problems. However, since this is not the case, structural changes in the food production and distribution systems are essential. An important solution is protecting smaller farmers from the manipulation of capital and markets by those who have amassed wealth. In the United States this requires a more dispersed ownership of productive farm land. While increased relief supplies and food reserves will relieve the desperate need for more equitably distributed food throughout the world, these are only short-term solutions. Even increased agricultural production will be of little value if there is no change in the marketing and distribution system. "The real issues of world hunger are found in the structure of control over food and resources, especially land and capital that are needed to produce food." Addressing these issues is more difficult and more controversial. It is also more critical and fundamental in solving the world hunger problem.[14]

The concentration of land and resource ownership, particularly in the hands of energy, timber, and railroad conglomerates, and the increasing development of intensive energy-dependent industrialized corporate agriculture demonstrates a second myth regarding land use that is operative in the United States today. That myth states that bigger is better.

For bigger to be better it would have to be proven that life-sustaining resources could be produced in greater quantities for the benefit of the common good at cheaper prices with less damage to the total environment and with conservation of scarce resources than would be possible with more diversified and smaller operations. Evidence is surfacing every day that that is simply not the case.

II
LAND ABUSE

Corporate farmers are trapped in a vicious circle. Monoculture production requires greater use of inorganic fertilizers and pesticides which depletes the soil and increases the resistance to and the variety of pests. This leads to use of stronger chemicals in greater quantities further depleting the land, bringing more pests and more chemicals. Soil erosion is increased. Almost four billion tons of sediment are washed into tributary streams in the United States each year.

The streams themselves are polluted and choked with sediment and chemical run-off. The vital resource of water is threatened in other ways as well. Enormous irrigation projects are required to keep the industrialized farms of the western plains in operation. The water system of the Ogallala formation in the High Plains area of Texas, Oklahoma, New Mexico, Kansas, Colorado, and Nebraska already has been affected by uncritical use. Agricultural and other users in this area are pumping water from the regional basin fifty times faster than it can be recharged. Drops in the water level have been recorded from forty to fifty feet in Oklahoma and Kansas, and at the present rate of development it is estimated that fifty percent of the acquifier under the state of Kansas will be gone by the end of the century. Development in other plains states is following the same reckless pattern.[15]

Water supplies are also directly affected by mining operations. Strip mining in the West is particularly damaging to the scarce water supply. Water now committed to agriculture may be diverted for mining, power plant cooling, coal gasification, and coal slurry pipeline operations. The dry ranch lands of Wyoming and Montana depend on irrigated acreage to provide hay and winter feed for cattle grazing on more than seven million acres the rest of the year. Disruption of this delicate balance could destroy the cattle and sheep industries.[16]

Disruption of the water supply in the Green River area of Utah, Colorado and Wyoming also seriously brings into question the planned development of oil shale holdings. A study prepared by the Center for Science in the Public Interest concluded that oil shale development in the Colorado River Basin would seriously aggravate the problem of salinity in that river system and adversely affect the streams, lakes and springs of the upper basin. The water supply is already inadequate in drought years. Mining and processing of oil shale would turn a serious problem into a critical one.[17]

The water system in the Appalachian Mountains has already been nearly destroyed through coal development. The stripping of steep mountains leaves a wide bench of exposed earth in a ring around the mountainside. Rain water collects on these strip benches and mixes with the sulphur laden coal residue of the mining operations. This creates ponds of sulfuric acid. The solid rock underbase of the stripped mountain prohibits absorption. The ponds expand until finally they spill over the mountainsides, turning creeks and streams into acidic baths. Leakage from improperly drained deep mines creates the same problem.

Through stripping, the land itself is destroyed. The Geological Survey estimated in 1970 that we had already stripped away 1.6 million acres of land, and that was before the onset of the energy crisis and the real boom in the strip mining industry. Seventy percent of the strippable reserves lie in states west of the Mississippi, and since that coal is more easily recovered than coal in the steep hills of Appalachia, expansion of western stripping is obvious. Illinois is already losing 6,000 acres of agricultural land to stripping per year. Studies question whether that land can ever be returned to original agricultural productivity.[18]

The timber industry also contributes its share to the abuse of land. In recent years clear-cutting practices have become widespread. Clear-cutting is the total leveling of a forest area rather than the selective cutting of mature, large, or dead trees. This practice is economically practical in the short-run because it requires less labor and less skill. A single piece of large equipment can replace a number of men.

Clear-cut land is difficult to regenerate and strict management is required if the soil of exposed areas is to be protected until reforestation takes hold. In the absence of such careful attention, clear-cutting in mountainous areas has contributed to increased flooding, soil erosion and further siltation of streams and creeks. In Appalachian areas it often happens that the surface rights to land are controlled by timber companies while the mineral rights are in the hands of energy conglomerates. Clear-cutting of these forest areas preceded the stripping of the mountains for coal. The double damage inflicted only intensifies the environmental catastrophe.

When viewing the destruction of the land, it is not difficult to understand why President Carter would warn in his inaugural address that bigger is not necessarily better. It is also not necessarily more efficient.

A 1972 USDA report found that maximum farm efficiency is generally achieved "at a relatively small size of operation and remains more or less constant through the very large size range."[19] More recently researchers from the Center for the Biology of Natural Systems at Washington University compared midwestern farms using organic methods with farms of comparable size using commercial fertilizers and pesticides. The study showed that organic farmers were making net incomes equal to the conventional farmers while using only one-third as much fossil fuel energy. The potentialities of smaller-scale, less energy-intensive agricultural production, however, are still largely unexplored in the U.S. Land grant universities, the USDA Cooperative Extension Service and federal agricultural experiment stations have been the bulwark of huge agribusiness operations. If the resources of this research and information distribution system were turned to the development of small-scale organic farming, even greater productivity would follow.

Bigness in the energy industry works directly against efficient and environmentally safe production. Further, the wealth and power of the industry has been sufficiently strong to block serious development of non-fossil fuels. The heart of the problem is the monopolistic holding of most sources of energy by the same few oil industry giants. The price of one fuel affects the prices of other fuels.

Presently, natural gas prices are regulated. Oil prices are more fluid. When oil prices are high it is not profitable to produce gas. If, in order to give incentive to production, gas prices are raised, coal production is affected. Coal can be converted to gas, though this would be at a higher price than natural gas. If, however, gas prices are allowed to rise, it will then be profitable to convert coal to gas. This will lead to increased stripping of Western coal to feed coal gasification plants. When oil, gas, and coal reserves are owned by the same company, it is obvious that production of one will be played off against the others to achieve the highest profit. Shortages are created simply by an unwillingness to produce whatever fuel would be at the relatively lower rate. This implies no conspiracy. All that is entailed is the maximization of profits. Industry executives would call it good business.[20]

Fear raised by shortages makes it easier to argue for deregulation of gas prices, increased coal production requiring very limited regulation of strip mining, easement of EPA air pollution standards, the opening of federal energy reserves to commercial development and tax incentives for energy investment.

III
POLICIES ENCOURAGING CONCENTRATION AND ABUSE OF LAND

Here a third false myth comes into play. That myth states that government tax policy is a method for redistributing the wealth of the country for the common good. On the contrary, the tax system in particular contributes to the concentration of wealth and ownership of land. The following are some examples of law that positively foster concentration of land ownership and/or land abuse.

Capital Gains: Profit made from the sale of appreciated investments are taxed at only half of regular income. This is an obvious factor in land speculation. Also, since almost all income from timber sales is treated as a capital gain, this loophole has provided an incentive for amassing huge timber acreage.

Tax Shelter for Land Purchase: If one borrows money to purchase land, the interest on that loan can be deducted from federal taxes. This encourages speculation because land can then be purchased with a small cash outlay and a loan. When sold, any profit from the transaction would only be taxed at the capital gains rate.

Tax-Loss Farming: Losses from farm operation can be deducted from federal income tax. Corporations are therefore encouraged to purchase agricultural land and operate it at a loss which can then be written off their profits in other divisions. Not only does this add to the process of corporate ownership of land, it also destroys the small farmer who must operate at a profit and cannot compete with tax-loss farming.[21]

Underassessment of Land: In many areas large corporate land holdings are grossly undervalued for tax purposes. In Doddridge County, West Virginia, for example, a 12,068 acre tract of land is valued at one dollar per acre. The tax per acre in 1974 came to two cents. This is not an uncommon example. The same situation exists throughout the country, whether one is talking about coal land in Appalachia, oil land in Texas, or timber land in Georgia or Maine.[22]

With the tax on land so pitifully low, land is a good investment for companies with huge cash flows. Since land is reassessed so infrequently, its purchase is a good hedge against inflation. Nobody is making new land. There will never be a glut on the market. Add this to the capital gains loophole when the land is eventually sold and sound business practice would practically force extensive land purchase.

Non-Taxation of Energy and Mineral Resources: Too often mineral holdings are not taxed at all. Because these are nonrenewable resources and are therefore depletable, they should be taxed *before* they are used. Mineral rich lands are often held in enormous tracts because the mineral wealth itself is not taxed. This practice prohibits development of alternative uses of the land, while at the same time it cuts income to local communities. It is then nearly impossible to diversify the economy of some areas. If anti-trust action could be applied to monopolistic land holding (a monopoly that stops competitive use of the land) it may be possible to break the back of the dependency syndrome in chronically poor areas such as Appalachia.

In addition to favorable tax laws, corporate ownership is also supported by acquiescence in the face of massive violations both of the letter and the intent of some laws.

The Railroad Land Grant Contracts: In the late 1800's Congress gave approximately 130 million acres of land (eight percent of the total U.S. land area) to the railroads. Most of these grants were made under specific contracts, requiring, among other things, (a) that the railroads could not extract for sale timber or minerals from the granted land, and (b) that after the railroads were constructed, the patented land should then be sold to settlers at prices between $1.25 and $2.50 per acre. Some railroad land was recovered in the late nineteenth and early twentieth centuries. Congress enacted legislation in 1940 to wipe out remaining railroad land grants. Despite that legislation, however, railroads still hold more than twenty million acres from which they are reaping tremendous incomes from timber and mineral rights.[23]

The Treaty of Guadalupe Hidalgo: The United States pledged in this treaty, ending the Mexican-American War, to uphold the rights of Chicano land holders in the formerly Mexican-held territory. That treaty was totally ignored. The *ejidos* of the Chicano *pueblos* were soon overrun with speculators and land grabbers. The Chicano people are still fighting for return of their land.

Indian Treaties: Similarly, the history of U.S. treaties with American Indian tribes is a history of land confiscation. Bad treaties, broken treaties and outright theft have wrenched from the American Indian what had been a commonly held and commonly respected resource.

The Reclamation Act of 1902: This act was designed to provide federally subsidized irrigation water to resident farmers whose tracts did not exceed 320 acres for couples or 160 acres for individuals. Wholesale violations have gone unprosecuted for years. A notable example of the corruption of this law is the Westlands Water District in California. "Farmers" there include Southern Pacific Railroad and Standard Oil of California. These absentee owners control thousands of acres in open violation of the law. The Bureau of Reclamation, by default if nothing else, is a party to the crime.[24]

Strip Mine Regulation and Reclamation Laws: State strip mine laws are rarely properly enforced. No federal strip mine law exists. The Center for Science in the Public Interest evaluated enforcement and reclamation programs in Kentucky, West Virginia and Pennsylvania. Its report, "Enforcement of Strip Mining Laws," cites instance after instance in which the regulatory bodies bend to the influence of the companies they are to regulate.[25]

Anti-Trust Laws: Anti-trust legislation is so cumbersome and there is such a "big industry" bias within government that the growth of monopolies has gone unabated. Both vertical and horizontal integration of two vital industries, food and energy, is progressing at a rapid rate.

The sad fact is that none of this story is new. While the issue of ecology has seeped into the national consciousness, that consciousness is only beginning to focus on the critical pressure point of land ownership. Somehow the issue of land, its use and abuse and needed reform, has been relegated to a "rural issue."

A mental image I have is that of rural people drowning in a violent storm just off the coast. Their cries for help go unheeded. The urban dwellers, crowded along the shore, are busily trying to keep the growing seepage of water from undermining the castles they are building in the sand. So great is their concentration, so great their own needs, that they fail to realize that the cries from the sea are also warnings of the tidal wave that is about to engulf them and their crumbling castles.

IV

Alternatives and Recommendations

Gloomy as this picture is, there are emerging several practical alternatives as well as a refined list of clear and precise needed policy changes. These suggestions have been urged again and again, principally by rural organizations. Among a number of fine organizations, the following have been particularly concerned with land and agricultural reform.

The National Catholic Rural Life Conference (Des Moines, Iowa) for half a century has been a voice crying in the wilderness. NCRLC's monthly magazine *Catholic Rural Life* continually and critically examines the questions of land, taxes, energy and agricultural abuse. This chapter constitutes somewhat of a synopsis of *Catholic Rural Life* for the past eighteen months. In-depth, detailed discussion of all the points raised here can be found in those issues.

The recently formed national rural caucus, Rural America, Inc. (Washington, D.C.) has also strongly stated a well-integrated national agenda gleaned from the long-standing efforts of its broad-based membership. National Land for People, an organization based in Fresno, California, but with national concerns, has concentrated specifically on the question of land reform, while the Agribusiness Accountability Project (Washington, D.C.) has done extensive research on the food industry.

Several proposals to prevent concentrated ownership of land are:

The Family Farm Anti-Trust Act: Since 1932 North Dakota has limited corporate farming. A national bill with similar provisions was introduced in Congress in 1975 but failed to get a hearing. The major provisions of a family farm act include (a) capital limitations, (b) control limitations, and (c) share limitations. Corporations, under a typical law, must have no more than twenty percent of capital input coming from operations outside of the farming effort. Control is exercised by allowing only family farm corporations or specially authorized corporations to engage in agriculture. The number of shareholders and the class of shareholders are usually limited. For instance, in most cases, shareholders must be real people, not other corporations. Adoption of a national family farm act would insure the return of agriculture to farmers and would break up the food monopolies.[26]

The Young Farmers Homestead Act: The Canadian province of Saskatchewan three years ago established a Land Bank Commission. The function of the commission was to purchase farms from retiring farmers and then to lease them at low cost to young farmers with the option of later purchase. The purpose of the land bank system is to remove the heavy burden of land payments and mortgage interests from farmers struggling to begin operations. They could then concentrate on investments in machinery, livestock and other farm necessities. In the United States, where good farm land sells for an average $1000 per acre, it is becoming increasingly impossible for anyone except huge agri-business corporations to sustain that kind of capital investment. A land bank system is needed here to prevent the continued trend toward agricultural monopoly. *The Young Farmers Homestead Act,* modeled on the Saskatchewan plan, was introduced in Congress in October, 1975. It received only two days of hearings before it was killed. Adoption of a land banking program however, would provide a workable solution to the concentration of land problem. It can be easily integrated into the present socio-economic structures of rural America without disrupting the system while at the same time setting a new direction for ownership of farm land.[27]

Community Land Trusts: Renewed interest has grown recently in the concept of a community land trust. Instead of private ownership, community ownership for the common good is emphasized. A community land trust has several basic provisions. First, it is *land* that is held in common. Buildings and other improvements on the land belong to the lease-holder. Lease-holders usually pay no rent for the land other than a contribution to upkeep and taxes. Second, the leasee is protected by assurance of a long-term lease, usually ninety-nine years and renewable. Third, the land itself is protected by compliance with the charter provisions which usually stipulate conservation practices. A final feature of the community land trust is that it removes land from the speculative market. Trust land cannot be rented, mortgaged or sold. Trusts usually require the leasee to live on the land. This perpetuates the principle that land belongs to those who use it and care for it. Land is not treated as a commodity. Absentee holding of land is abolished.[28]

Specific recommendations include:

• Complete a national inventory of land and resource ownership by 1979. (We simply do not have any systematic national data on who owns the land.)

- Restrict corporate farming through the adoption of a Family Farm Act at both the state and federal level.
- Develop a farm leasing program for young farmers with provision for purchase at low cost with long-term, low-interest credit.
- Curtail land speculation through the elimination of capital gains, tax loss farming and other tax loopholes.
- Enact a system of progressive property tax at the state level whereby the more land a person or corporation owns, the higher the rate of tax. This should be keyed to the actual number of acres owned rather than assessed valuation.
- Ban strip mining.
- Enforce the 160 acre limit and residency requirement in federal reclamation areas.
- Require railroads to forfeit land, particularly mineral holdings and agricultural land retained in violation of original grant agreements.
- Vigorously enforce existing anti-trust legislation and extend anti-trust laws to include monopolized holding of land.
- Prohibit oil companies (or any fuel company) from owning competitive energy sources.
- Break up the vertical integration of the oil industry separating production from refinement.
- Break up the vertical integration in agribusiness and encourage farmer-to-consumer marketing wherever possible.
- Concentrate federal resources on the development of non-fossil fuels.
- Fund research that develops alternative energy resources and that develops organic farming methods.
- Prioritize these concerns within the land grant college-cooperative extension system and tie funding to such priority programming.
- Enact state severance taxes on oil, coal, timber, uranium.
- Give tax credits for the cost of installing solar heating units in private homes.
- Reduce energy consumption.

V

MORAL IMPLICATIONS

To act morally is to act according to one's concept of what is right and just. More and more as we experience the world as limited, interconnected, and fragile, we come to the moral realization that to hoard, destroy and waste the earth is to destroy life, and to the conviction that this destruction is obviously and blatantly wrong.

Several principles of stewardship emerge as self-evident. They are:

. . . the earth belongs to everyone,

. . . to share and to cherish,

. . . to use wisely and sparingly,

. . . and to renew and preserve for future generations.

Abuse of these principles results in:

. . . concentration of land ownership and therefore concentration of wealth and power for the few with concomitant poverty and powerlessness for the many.

. . . gross consumption of non-renewable resources, and

. . . disruption of the ecological balance.

Most of us have been schooled in a tradition that has viewed morality in personal terms. Sin has tended to be described as personal transgressions. Another dimension of sin, however, is social sin. There are two ways to talk about social sin. First, it can be defined in terms of its object. That is, social sin is the evil done by one or several persons that adversely affects society. This is certainly a dimension of social sin but it is still very close to personal sin in that it involves the deliberate acts of conscious individuals.

Another way to define social sin is in terms of the subject. That is, evil consequences are produced by the very structures and institutions of the society. There is no guilt in the ordinary sense. It seems very helpful to make this distinction. For to speak of sin only in terms of personal responsibility leads to the conclusion that the evil that exists results from sinful individuals and this precludes the need to examine the social institutions themselves.

Now, obviously, there are both personal and social dimensions to sin. But there is need to balance the notion of personal sin with an equally clear understanding of the necessity to examine the social institutions themselves in moral terms.

Commitment to stewardship of land implies personal responsibility in choice of life-style. It also requires critical examination of unjust social institutions and the denunciation of those institutions as sinful where injustices exist. That is, institutions that contribute to a grossly unbalanced distribution of land and its life-essential resources, that contribute to destruction of the delicate interrelationships of the ecological system, and that contribute to the depletion of critical and non-renewable resources are not just unfortunate political, social and economic arrangements; they are sinful in themselves.

NOTES

1. Peter Barnes, ed., *The People's Land: A Reader on Land Reform in the United States* (Emmaus, Pennsylvania: Rodale Press, 1975), p. x.

2. Peter Barnes and Larry Casalino, *Who Owns The Land?* (Berkeley, California: Center for Rural Studies, 1972), pp. 6-7.

3. Tom Miller, *Who Owns West Virginia?* (Huntington, West Virginia: The Huntington Publishing Company, 1974), pp. 1-3.

4. Barnes, *The People's Land,* p. 52.

5. *Ibid.,* p. 45.

6. Frederick J. Perella, Jr., *Poverty in American Democracy: A Study of Social Power* (Washington, D.C.: U.S. Catholic Conference, 1974), p. 101.

7. Angus McDonald, *Interlocking Oil: Big Oil Ties With Other Corporations* (Washington, D.C.: Center for Science in the Public Interest, 1974), p. 51.

8. John F. Stacks, *Stripping* (San Francisco: Sierra Club, 1972), pp. 125-128.

9. A. V. Krebs, "Corporate Farm Activity Documented in New Study," *Catholic Rural Life,* Vol. 24, No. 11 (November 1975), p. 8.

10. Stephen Bossi, "Bill Would Curb Growing Corporate Food Control," *Catholic Rural Life,* Vol. 24, No. 11 (November 1975), p. 19.

11. "Six States Report More Than 9,000 Corporations in Farming and Ranching," *Catholic Rural Life,* Vol. 26, No. 1 (January 1977), pp. 3-5.

12. *Ruralamerica,* Vol. I, No. 8 (May 1976), p. 4.

13. Joseph F. Brooks, "Loss of Black Owned Land Continues in Rural South," *Catholic Rural Life,* Vol. 25, No. 3 (March 1976), p. 11.

14. Stephen Bossi, "Structural Problems Are The Critical Issue in Solving Hunger Dilemma," *Catholic Rural Life,* Vol. 25, No. 4 (April 1976), pp. 3-4.

15. Sr. Helen Vinton, "Irrigation Threatens Plains States Water," *Catholic Rural Life,* Vol. 25, No. 3 (March 1976), p. 9.

16. Roger Blobaum, "Energy Development Takes Water and Land—Can We Afford To Pay the Price?" *Catholic Rural Life,* Vol. 25, No. 1 (January 1976), p. 11.

17. Angus McDonald, *Shale Oil: An Environmental Critique* (Washington, D.C.: Center for Science in the Public Interest, 1974), p. 60.

18. John C. Doyle, Jr. *Strip Mining in the Corn Belt* (Washington, D.C.: Environmental Policy Institute, 1976).

19. Susan Sechler and Jim Hightower, "Big Business Down on the Farm," *Journal of Current Social Issues,* Vol. 11, No. 8 (Fall 1974), p. 10.

20. Stacks, *Stripping,* p. 130.

21. Perella, *Poverty in American Democracy,* p. 125.

22. Miller, *Who Owns West Virgina?* p. 23.

23. Barnes and Casalino, *Who Owns the Land?* p. 3.

24. *Ruralamerica,* Vol. 1, No. 8 (May 1976), p. 6.

25. Albert J. Fritsch, S.J. *Enforcement of Strip Mining Laws* (Washington, D.C.: Center for Science in the Public Interest, 1975).

26. Curt Sorteberg, "Several Midwest States Curb Corporate Farming," *Catholic Rural Life,* Vol. 24, No. 11 (November 1975), p. 4.

27. Roger Blobaum, "Plan for Young People Who Want To Farm Is Introduced in Congress," *Catholic Rural Life,* Vol. 24, No. 12 (December 1975), pp. 17-18.

28. Barnes, *The People's Land,* pp. 215-216.

World Grain Reserve

Brennon Jones

Stewardship of agricultural resources should, if nothing else, insure two things: that all people have access to adequate supplies of food at a reasonable price, and that those who produce our food be guaranteed a sufficient return on their production to be an incentive for them to continue to produce. Neither of these requirements is now being adequately met, and the cost is periodic hardship to producers, consumers, and particularly hungry people. Our lack of stewardship is reflected in what we have allowed to happen to the world's grain supplies in recent years with the extremes of death-provoking shortages in 1972-74, and price depressing surpluses in 1977. But the effects are seen in other crops as well, and are routinely the same—periodic excessively high prices, periodic disastrously low prices, with fluctuations between extremes of oversupply and undersupply. Consider the two recent examples of beef and sugar.

Boom and Bust

In 1973, consumers were disturbed by the high price of beef, which they boycotted. Yet by mid-1974, the depressed prices beef producers were receiving were symbolized by the random shooting of cattle, witnessed on TVs across the country. Alternately consumers had been priced out of the market, and producers were unable to break even with the prices they were receiving for their beef.

A similar "boom and bust" price cycle occurred with sugar. Consumers boycotted it in the fall of 1974, when the price for a pound of sugar peaked at 69¢. Yet raw sugar prices in early 1977 had plunged to barely 7¢ a pound, leaving the poor producing countries, many of which rely heavily on sugar for foreign earnings, wondering how they would pay their debts and meet even their most basic needs. Once again, both consumers and producers were alternately hurt.

While instability in supply and price is bad enough in crops such as beef and sugar—such fluctuations are deadly when they occur in grain—the staple food for most of the world's population.

Avoiding this situation is, at its heart, a question of stewardship: how best to provide for the lean years of food scarcity, and how best to avoid the extreme fluctuations in price that buffet both consumers and producers. Both require reserves.

Providing for periods of scarcity is as basic as Joseph's wise advice to the Pharaoh that food reserves should be held against the seven years of famine. Avoiding the extreme fluctuations in price that hurt both consumers and producers also calls for reserves, but ones that can be used to provide stability to the price of grain by releasing grain on the market when prices are excessively high and placing grain in storage when prices are excessively low. The alternative is the current situation in which some periodically profit, but always at the expense of others.

One Kansas farmer exclaimed some time ago, when prices for his crops were high, that the agricultural "free market system is great as it allows farmers to be just like that guy in Las Vegas. We take the gambles, but we have the chance to win big on occasion."

It's true enough, but at whose cost? At those times when farmers do "win big" the food costs for consumers and hungry people are so high as to price many of them out of the market. And consumers only get "bargain prices" if the farmer is receiving prices so low that they don't adequately cover his production cost. Ironically at the end of 1976, that gambling Kansas farmer was singing a different tune as he sat on grain surpluses that had pushed average U.S. farm prices to the lowest level in relation to other U.S. prices since 1936. Good stewardship demands a negotiation between producers, consumers, and the hungry to insure that each benefits, but not at the expense of the others. The issue is of such importance to all people that it is morally imperative to succeed in reconciling the real and apparent conflicts between these groups.

Who Needs Reserves?

The need for reserves for hungry people is perhaps the most pressing and certainly the most obvious: sufficient reserves insure both that there is adequate food to provide assistance to mal-nourished people and that the price of food on the commercial market doesn't go so high as to price the poor buyer out of the market. Recent history demonstrates the failure of current policies.

During the 1965-66 marketing year, poor crops in the Soviet Union, South Asia, and elsewhere created a demand for grain that was thirty-five million tons greater than total world production. Because world reserves at that time were ample, the needed grain was provided both in food aid and through the normal commercial markets, and with a negligible effect on prices.

But in the 1972-73 market year, the situation was quite different. World reserves had been allowed to dwindle, just at a time when unusual weather conditions had reduced world production by some twenty-three million tons. The harsh competition for available food caused grain prices to treble and quadruple. Wheat rose from $60 a ton to $200, and rice from $130 to over $500 a ton.

Even at those prices, the poor countries were still dependent for much of their food on commercial purchases. Such price increases were a heavy burden for the average third world citizen who even in normal times spends as much as sixty to eighty percent of his income on food. And they proved crippling for a nation such as India that was forced to spend more than $500 million of its own scarce capital on U.S. food purchases, when the money was desperately needed for India's critical longer-term food production, population planning, and development programs.

And just as commercial food prices skyrocketed, the quantity of food assistance provided to the developing nations shrunk. The reason is that U.S. food aid provided under the PL-480 program is bought at current market prices; thus at the times it is most needed, when food prices are high, the U.S. food aid dollar buys less, and the U.S. government is reluctant to make large purchases for fear it will push the U.S. domestic price for consumers too high. True to form, total U.S. PL-480 food aid shipments dropped from the 9 million ton level in fiscal year 1972 when prices were normal to a low of 3.3 million ton level in 1974 when prices were high. The decrease meant the difference between life and death for many.

Recently available data documents the increase in death rates during the 1972-74 period. In one rural district in Bangladesh, Matlab Bazar, death rates were directly linked to food scarcity. Without adequate food aid in 1974, Matlab Bazar's death rate soared, suggesting a nationwide increase in deaths of 300,000. Data from India indicates a similar increase in death rate in 1972—with more than 800,000 lives lost in the states of Bihar, Orissa, and Uttar Pradesh alone. And such statistics do not reflect the millions whose minds and bodies have been permanently damaged by the hunger they suffered during those years.

While the benefit of reserves for the poor and hungry in times of shortage is clear, an equally good case can be made that well-managed reserves serve their interest in times of over-supply as well. Grain surpluses in the exporting countries inevitably induce farmers who are saddled with depressed prices for their crops to seek two solutions, both of which are potentially detrimental to the poor countries. First, they aggressively try to sell their cheap grain to foreign markets in order to eliminate domestic surpluses, and, second, they march on Washington, urging that their surpluses be unloaded through the PL-480 food aid program. The effect all too often is for leaders in developing countries to depend on cheap American food to feed their people rather than concentrating on the promotion of their own indigenous agricultural production. Typically, they reason that it is easier to accept U.S. food aid, or to buy American food at bargain prices for their large urban popula-tions, than to make the politically tougher decision of guaranteeing their own farmers the incentives to produce. Consequently, the cheap imported food depresses market prices, and the indigenous farmer, who finds he is receiving insufficient money for his crops to cover his costs, simply stops producing for the market. Govern-ment Accounting Office (GAO) studies bear this out, with one, which was especially critical of the U.S. food aid program, stating that "bulk quantities of food on concessional terms (such as the $27 billion worth provided by the U.S.) have adversely affected production in developing countries by keeping down prices, and by permitting governments to postpone needed agricultural reforms." The result is an unhealthy dependence on imported food, leading to the poor being denied adequate supplies just at the time they are needed most, and to developing country farmers being denied the opportunity to pursue self-reliant national food production, even though the ability is there.

Farmers' Stake in Reserves

While many U.S. farmers are wary of reserves, they are for them no less important. Farmer wariness stems from the effects of massive stocks that were held in the United States during the 1950's and 1960's. While the farmer's problem today is the effect of temporary oversupply and undersupply situations, then it was one of post-World War II domestic farm productivity having increased so rapidly that supply had far outpaced demand. Farm income stagnated year after year, and the government became the customer of last resort, holding prices up to a level that would help keep farmers in business.

Although they kept prices from collapsing, the government financing schemes didn't make the average farmer rich. From 1960 to 1969, for example, the per-capita disposable income of farm people averaged only 65 percent of non-farm people. Unfortunately, however, the support prices were high enough to spur continued overproduction, which meant that prices consistently stayed down near the support level. The price support system originally designed to help the farmer had backfired because of the large surpluses generated. Discouraged by low earnings, many farmers left the farm forever.

Now, however, U.S. farmers are at the mercy of wildly fluctuating grain prices due to both periodic surpluses and shortages. And while such fluctuations may benefit the strongest market speculator, they frustrate the family farmer's plans for orderly investment (and consequently also affect the enterprises from which he purchases his farm equipment and agricultural imputs).

Many highly productive farmers have failed for lack of capital margins sufficient to weather periods of severe downward price swings. And grain producers are not the only ones to suffer. "Boom and bust" prices hit other food sectors particularly hard, especially millers and processors of grain, and livestock producers who are dependent on grain to feed their cattle, milk cows, hogs and chickens.

Presently, U.S. farmers are victimized by both oversupply and undersupply situations. In the absence of reserves, and without adequate government supports, in recent years farmers have looked to expanding foreign export markets to sell much of their produce. While the markets were strong during the crisis years of 1972-74, good harvests worldwide in 1976 mean that those strong markets are no longer there. Thus, U.S. farmers, laboring under a government policy of no reserves, are stuck with large grain surpluses, and market prices too low for them to cover their production costs.

And not only the farmers are taking a beating, but so is their land. In pursuit of what they thought were expanding foreign markets, farmers have produced at maximum and sometimes ecologically unsound levels. Not since the "dust-bowl" days have farmers been as worried about valuable topsoil blowing away. Much of the problem has been aggravated by farmers chopping down wind-protective hedge-rows that had been sown in the 1930's in order to increase their planted acreage. If surpluses were in reserve, the grain prices farmers received would be more stable, and farmers would not be pushed to the excess of planting hedge-row to hedge-row.

In the absence of reserves, and in periods of short-supply and high prices, farmers are again hurt, this time by export controls clamped on U.S. grain. Embargoes were placed on U.S. soybeans in 1973, "prior government approval" export controls were placed on grain sales in the fall of 1974, and a moratorium on sales to Russia was established in August 1975, costing farmers millions of dollars in lost sales. Reserves avoid the need for politically and economically disruptive export controls that frustrate importers and exporters alike, and insure continuity of supply to foreign markets.

The instability that has hit the American farm community in

recent years due to the lack of grain reserves is affecting rural America in general, farmers have suffered with unpredictable and wildly fluctuating incomes year to year. Some have gone bankrupt, and most are heavily in debt, with only the largest ultimately able to survive. The impact this is having on rural America is essentially a stewardship question. As family farmers are forced to move out, increasingly it is the large corporate farms that take their place, consolidating landholding in the process. Many large corporate farms are owned by absentee landlords who live in the city of their corporate headquarters and depend on farm managers. They tend to have no need for "Main Street" America with its churches, schools and businesses, for they spend their time and income outside the rural community. The financial and social decline of these stagnating communities over a period of time is predictable if present trends are allowed to continue.

Consumers Benefit

For consumers in general, the need for reserves is equally obvious: they insure continuous supplies of food at reasonable prices, and they restrain other general price increases in the economy. According to the Committee for Economic Development, the lack of reserves played the crucial role in the thirty-five percent rise in the food component of the consumer price index during 1973-74. Such sharp consumer price increases seldom decrease as grain prices decline—and, in a ripple effect, they spur general price and wage increases throughout the rest of the economy. The burden of price increases then falls heaviest on the poorest of consumers, and particularly those on fixed incomes. Ironically, those farmers who benefited temporarily from the skyrocketing grain prices are ultimately hurt when grain prices drop again, and yet they are stuck paying more because of the price increases of their farm imputs.

Criteria for Managing Reserves

The difficulties of controlling and managing reserves are real, and ultimately sound stewardship demands that effective reserves be designed to insure these things: 1. That the United States does not end up paying all of the cost, nor having all the control, of the world's reserves. 2. That farmers of the world should not end up unjustly carrying the burden of cost for reserves which benefit the world community, since the essence of good stewardship demands that farmers have the necessary incentives to produce. 3. That reserves should support rather than deter the movement toward greater self-reliance in the developing nations; and therefore not be dumped on the poor nations. 4. That reserves should not be open to manipulation or used as a means to depress prices for short-term political advantage.

In the final analysis, while the problems are difficult, the cost of not having reserves is economic, social, and political disaster, leading to the sacrifice of additional millions of lives to scarcity. This was acknowledged at the time of the World Food Conference in November 1974 when the nations of the world agreed to build reserves as a part of the "International Undertaking on Food Security." The objective was "to ensure the availability at all times of adequate world supplies of basic foodstuffs . . . so as to avoid acute shortages in the event of widespread crop failures or natural disasters, sustain a steady expansion of production and reduce fluctuations in production and prices."

But nations have been slow to implement the plan, and in the face of future supply and demand uncertainties their inaction amounts to folly. On the supply side, the world is no longer assured unlimited amounts of water, arable land, or energy. All are diminishing and are becoming increasingly more costly. On the demand side, population is continuing to grow with a consequent additional annual need of at least thirty million tons of grain. And as nations develop, their increasing consumption of red meat requires more and more grain for livestock feeding.

Add to the supply-demand equation two other uncertainties: one is weather, about which the only certainty is that we know precious little. Long-term natural shifts in weather patterns have occurred repeatedly in the past and are likely again. Human factors such as the increase in atmospheric carbon dioxide from industrial expansion, and dust from mechanized agriculture and overgrazing, are now changing patterns as well. And climatic surprises such as the record cold experienced in the United States in the winter of 1976-77 should prod us into preparing for the inevitable lean years.

The other uncertainty is the unlikelihood of new breakthroughs in agricultural technology. Agricultural scientists are hard at work attempting to unlock the secrets of nitrogen fixation, photosynthesis, and genetic engineering. But progress is slow and agricultural research funds are diminishing when they should be increasing. While impressive strides have been made in agricultural production particularly with doubling in U.S. output over the last three decades, it was achieved not so much through scientific breakthroughs as through new techniques for utilization of what was then considered cheap energy, fossil fuel, in fertilizer and in mechanized agriculture. The energy is no longer cheap, nor are new breakthroughs likely to come as easily in the future.

Even in the face of such uncertainties in future food production, government leaders have been myopic in preparing for the longer-term needs of their citizens, and have taken only piecemeal action to buffer consumers and producers from the insecurities of present agricultural supply and price fluctuations. Ultimately, it will be plain people—on the farms, in the cities, and in the churches—who must become the stewards of their citizenship on behalf of all who produce and consume food. Real stewardship will require nothing less than a lot of sharing and tough negotiation between farmers, consumers, and hungry people to insure adequate supplies of food for all, and a fair return for the farmer, so that each benefits, but not at the expense of the other.

Stewardship and the Food, Energy, Environment Triangle

Eric G. Walther

What Is Stewardship?

Stewardship is living in dynamic equilibrium. Life is conducted so that the world is handed from one generation to the next in just as good condition or better. Because of our increased environmental awareness in recent years, it is clear that stewardship requires a style of life that doesn't permanently degrade the environment supporting us. We need to learn that our environment provides us with all the resources necessary for life, including life itself. From our environment we get the air we need for oxygen, the water we drink, and the plants and other animals we eat. From our environment we also get all the materials we fabricate into clothes, shelter, public works, appliances, books, and all the other things that make life comfortable or interesting.

Stewardship requires the concept of group. It is a life-style for the common good and requires some self-denial of individualistic greed. Here are the ethics and values that occupy much of the attention of religion. Stewardship means we limit our individual greed so that others, including people still unborn, can share in limited resources. There is a strong future orientation to stewardship, in contrast to the aspect of greed that emphasizes "now." Stewardship does not prevail in contemporary societies. The current United States society certainly relegates stewardship to a low position in guiding our individual and group actions. Most people in the United States today are more concerned with gathering unto themselves all the comforts and luxuries they can buy on credit than they are with providing their children and future generations with a beautiful world containing sufficient resources for a good life.

Fortunately, there still exist some examples of groups committed to stewardship. One example is the Hopi Indian tribe in northeastern Arizona. This group of six thousand individuals has a thousand-year tradition of living in harmony with their environment. They have exercised rigorous population control in order not to exceed the carrying capacity of their hard environment on several mesas looking over the Painted Desert. Their population was also limited by their ability to grow corn and other food in an arid environment. Dryland farming in northeastern Arizona doesn't yield much corn. One of their cities, Oraibi, has remained livable for one thousand years. This long habitation is a strong contrast with the decay rampant in most of our large old cities like New York.

Stewardship and Food

The stewardship of food means a two-way sharing of this resource with others. First is the sharing with others now alive on the face of the earth. Each person needs at least a certain amount of food to lead a healthy life. This amount varies with age, stature, and activity level. For example, an American adult needs 1,800-3,000 kilocalories of food energy per day and 44-78 grams of protein per day. In the United States, this requirement is easy to meet. In fact, we eat an average of 3,000 kilocalories per day and 90-97 grams of protein per day. Some of us eat even more in excess of the requirements while others are starving to death in our poor rural areas and urban ghettos. In other parts of the world, many more are not getting basic requirements. No wonder that many people in the poor world have stunted bodies and minds.

What we learn from the real world is that the usual guiding philosophy is greed, not stewardship. Greed is successfully carried out whenever the greedy people have the power to gather a disproportionate share of resources. When resources for the survival of all people in a group become scarce, stewardship declines and may completely disappear. In situations of extreme stress like ship and airplane wrecks, prisoner-of-war and concentration camps, many people completely abandon sharing the hardship and try to capture much more than an equal share of the available resources. Yet there are other people who continue to share resources even under great stress and fear for their survival.

There is some irony in the relationship between stewardship and wealth. A group of "rich" people with plenty of resources for all will often abandon stewardship and fight over possession of more than an equal share of the resources. In contrast, a group of "poor" people will often show an amazing degree of stewardship in their equal sharing of the available resources.

Those of us in middle-class America share our food reasonably well among our own family members. We share less well with the poor in our own nation, although we at least have food stamps and religious food relief efforts to carry out some sharing. We share even less with poor nations, despite the existence of food aid to nations when they have catastrophic famines. No reasonable food sharing by the United States can hope to eliminate totally the malnutrition existing among the four billion who presently populate the earth. There are just too many poorly fed people to expect even our food production to feed them all with good diets.

We might decry this state of affairs in the nutrition of the world's people, but it is linked to our political and economic systems. In our present system, people eat what they can buy. A greater stewardship in feeding people can only come from a profound change in the system of distributing wealth and all derived resources. Redistributing wealth is the same thing as redistributing power, and power will only be redistributed if the powerful see it in their best interest to do so or suddenly embrace the concept of sharing. In resource systems, redistributing power counters the basic biological pursuit of survival. The populations of species are held in check by competition from other species for the same resources. Different tree species compete for light entering a forest canopy. Insects, fungi, and weeds compete with us for our crops and cropland. Lions and other predator cats compete for the limited number of antelope, zebras, and other animals they can catch, kill, and eat.

Most of the four billion people in the world are closer to the survival level than middle-class Americans. Yet they may exhibit more stewardship than middle-class Americans in their sharing of scarce resources and the associated hardship. There seems to be some balance of competition for survival and cooperation for sharing in all reasonably stable societies, no matter how rich or poor they are. When the balance is lost to unrestrained competition, anarchy results.

Stewardship and Food Producing Resources

In order to apply stewardship to food, we have to apply it to the resources with which we produce food. The primary resources supporting food production are land, water, seed, and energy. Land was the traditional variable controlled by human management. As our population around the world increased, we cut down forests for farmland. Unfortunately, this trade-off has not been questioned thoroughly enough. Forests offer a tremendous bounty of both physical and psychological resources. They offer wilderness, recreation, lumber, erosion control, new soil, and water-holding capacity. We are finding out that the indiscriminate cutting and clearing of forests for farmland is becoming counterproductive in parts of the world. An example is the cutting of too many trees for firewood and construction in Nepal. The result is a loss of water-holding capacity in the upper watersheds of the Ganges, a great loss of soil to the uncontrolled runoff, and flooding of the lowlands in Bangladesh with its associated washing away of people living there. In order to achieve stewardship with respect to food and land, we will have to achieve an equilibrium distribution of land for farming, land for cities, land for mining, and land for forests and other natural ecosystems.

Stewardship of food requires the stewardship of water. Water is the prime climatic variable that determines crop yield. Only ten percent of the cropland around the world is irrigated, where we can manage the water input to the crop. The other ninety percent gets its water only from precipitation. The stewardship of water with respect to food means quality control. We need to control our other uses of water so that its quality is not degraded enough to hurt agriculture. Our record so far isn't good. Industrialization and urbanization have heavily polluted rivers in many parts of the world. First, we lost the ability to drink these polluted rivers; then we couldn't swim in them; and, finally, some rivers have become so polluted that they can't support any aquatic life nor even be treated chemically for municipal use. Obviously, there is not stewardship in any of these trends. Furthermore, we now know that industry and our other air polluting activities are acidifying our precipitation. This change is killing fish in fresh-water lakes. It may also be hurting crops slightly, but we don't know because of lack of study. Overall, stewardship of water for food will require finding an equilibrium use of water for all purposes so that one purpose doesn't ruin the water for other purposes.

Applying the concept of stewardship to seed for food plants is an entirely different situation. Here, the concept of equilibrium must be used in its dynamic form, not in its static form. Nowhere in this essay do I use equilibrium in its static form, but here the dynamic aspect becomes clearer. We are all evolving; however, humans evolve more slowly than most plant and animal species. If we were to stop our scientific evolution of new plant varieties and biocides, then soon we would find our crops eaten up by insects and disease before we could harvest. Change is the key to survival in this race between breeding new plant varieties resistant to insects and disease, and the evolution of the insects and disease to get around the effects of our biocides.

Stewardship of energy with respect to food requires some more discussion of the relationship between energy and food. First of all, food is energy. Food also possesses other important characteristics, including protein and vitamins. Yet, it is the ability of plants to fix solar energy by photosynthesis that allows any form of life on earth. Animals build their complexity on the energy foundation provided by plants. Nitrogen fixation to build amino acids and protein is run on the energy captured with which we subsidize the increased yield of crop plants. Much of the irrigation around the world is pumped ground-water rather than gravity-fed diversions from rivers. It takes a lot of energy to pump ground-water to the surface; hence, this type of irrigation can be viewed as another energy subsidy we provide to increase crop yield. Because food is a renewable resource, its stewardship is conceptually easy to understand. Stewardship of its energy inputs is not simple because much of this energy comes from fossil fuels that are non-renewable. It is difficult to apply stewardship to a resource that is disappearing. By definition, we must hand the next generation less of a non-renewable resource. Fortunately, not all energy sources are non-renewable, so we can now emphasize those energy sources that are more compatible with stewardship. An example is solar energy.

Stewardship and Energy

Applying stewardship to energy forces us to think more about renewable sources like solar energy, wind, hydropower, tides, wood, wave action, and photosynthesis. If we trace human history, then we can see our early dependence on wood burning for heating and cooking, and our never-ending dependence on photosynthesis for food. Only in the last one to two hundred years have we developed societies dependent on the non-renewable fossil fuels of coal, oil, and natural gas. During this brief love affair with fossil fuels, we have consumed them so quickly that the production of natural gas in the United States peaked in 1973 and the production of oil in the United States peaked in 1971. Since these peaks, we have produced less natural gas and oil. We have so depleted two of our three fossil fuels that we must now begin our return to renewable sources. In the next quarter century, we will equip many of our homes to capture sunlight for part of our heating and cooling needs. We will tap geothermal energy in several parts of the world. We may build wind generators and solar converters to produce electricity. We will explore thermal gradients in the oceans and wave action in the hope that these sources will be significant someday. Various municipalities around the nation are developing resource recovery programs, one part of which is the reclamation of the energy in the paper waste. Utilities can burn this paper waste along with coal and convert the energy into electricity. In India, animal manure and food waste is being composted in home units so as to capture the methane and use it for cooking and lighting.

Any type of recycling is consistent with stewardship because recycling conserves resources for the future. Further, any conservation of land, water, energy, and other earth resources helps minimize the environmental problems caused by resource extraction and use.

Stewardship and Environmental Quality

We have come full circle in our discussion of stewardship. We started with its definition in terms of dynamic equilibrium, so that we hand future generations a world at least as beautiful as was handed us. Environmental problems arise as we pursue food, energy, materials, and the final products of using energy and materials. Pollution is the result of leaky processes. If we could contain all the materials and energy we use in our activities, there would be no pollution. Perfect containment is impossible. Pollution is unacceptably high leakage of substances into the atmosphere, water, or soil. At low enough rates, leakage of substances can be satisfactorily absorbed and recycled by the environment. This process of dilution is within the carrying capacity of the environment. Pollution results when we exceed the carrying capacity of the environment for the injection of some substance. When this carrying capacity is exceeded, we have also violated a basic condition for stewardship of environmental quality.

Stewardship and Ownership

It is important to note that stewardship can be fulfilled or violated with both private and public ownership. Private ownership encourages the efficient use of resources for the owner's maximum profit. The owner tends to use his own resources carefully, but he cares less to apply stewardship to the resources of others, especially those in the public commons. For example, a power company will tend to use its coal efficiently without air pollution if that reduces its construction cost.

In contrast, public ownership can just as easily lead to the abuses termed "tragedy of the commons" by Garrett Hardin. A common example is the citizen who dumps his car ash tray in a public parking lot. He pollutes the public domain in order to clean his private domain. Air pollution is another example of fouling the public domain in order to reduce costs in private domains.

Conclusion

Although examples of stewardship exist, it is not a governing principle for most people. Stewardship requires a concern for the well-being of future generations as well as a concern for the well-being of all people alive now. Most of the four billion people alive now are not well fed, well clothed, well sheltered, well educated, well in health, or well in spirit. On top of this situation, we are currently adding somewhere between sixty-seven and ninety-two million more people to the earth each year. If we are to have any hope of sharing more equally the available resources so that each person has enough to live comfortably, then stewardship must be pursued as part of the pursuit of a more basic dynamic equilibrium. Two cases for future population are shown in Figure 1. Continuation of the present exponential growth of global population would lead to the "Big Bang" case, in which our global population would exhaust energy, food, environmental quality and other critical resources and plummet fast enough to induce chaos and anarchy in our societies. This case practices population control through increasing the death rate, a route universally loathed by the loved ones of those who die. The "Dynamic Equilibrium" case requires the realization that reduction of the birth rate is far preferable to widespread increases in the death rate, and that reducing the birth rate is essential to a more equal sharing of resources both with those people alive and those to come in the future. This would truly be global stewardship.

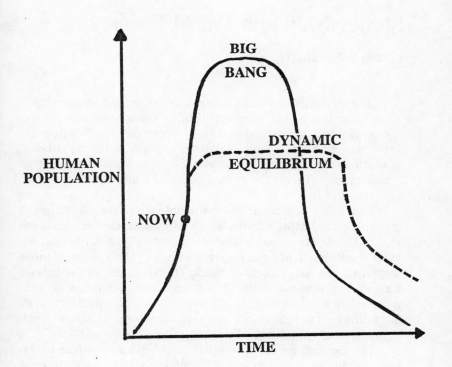

FIGURE 1

Stewardship and World Poverty

George S. Siudy, Jr.

Under no conditions can a world fully inhabited and carrying seven to ten billion people still offer rising standards to a minority and, at best, stagnation to everyone else. Whatever we plan or think . . . we shall meet the new restraints either with resentment, anger and revolt, or with dignity, patience and sharing. This is the critical point for Christian witness.[1]

Thirty-five degrees above the equator, a poverty curtain circles the globe. Most nations north of that curtain are industrialized. Most nations south of it are industrially underdeveloped. Most people north of the curtain are white or yellow. Most of those south of it are red, brown, or black. On both sides of the curtain whites dominate the political and economic existence of nonwhites. North of the curtain, the majority is affluent. South of it, more than one billion humans are destitute, illiterate, malnourished, and chronically ill.

This poverty curtain is new to humankind. Prior to the industrial revolution, most people were poor. But, by 1950, a great chasm had opened across the world: the ratio of income in industrial nations to that in non-industrial nations was 15 to 1. By 2000 A.D., it is expected to be 30 to 1.[2]

The communications network that permeates the modern world is carrying signals of affluence across the poverty curtain. Among the poor, these signals are generating a ferment manifest in the decolonizing of governments and nationalizing of resources, in guerrilla campaigns and terrorist actions, and in stiffening resistance to domination by outsiders.

Signals of poverty reach the affluent. On television, North

Americans and Europeans watch humans die of hunger in Bangladesh, India, and the Sahel. Consumer goods grow short—natural gas, petroleum, grain, meat, coffee—and shake the comfort of the complacent. In the face of an abyss of global poverty, ethically sensitive people ask: "What action is fitting for good stewards of the earth's resources?"

Measuring World Poverty

To measure world poverty is a formidable task. The data are of uneven quality. Some statistics are crude estimates, weighted to serve those who make them. Some income data include the value of non-monetary goods; some do not. Per capita income is usually derived by dividing a nation's gross domestic product by its population. But, since income is unevenly distributed throughout a nation, the poor are sure to have less income than per capita data report. Costs of living vary from one nation and region to another.

Global economists acknowledge difficulty with the data, but use them with caution and measure poverty in four ways: relative inequality of income, absolute poverty, differentiated economic and social factors, and nutrition.

For the United States, 1974 per capita income was $6,600. For twenty-six nations it was under $300. For an additional twenty-eight nations, it was less than $750. Of one hundred and five nations reporting, only twenty-five had per capita incomes over $2,000.[3] This *relative inequality of income* is not diminishing. World Bank economist Mahbub ul Haq observes that in the past two decades, in spite of industrial growth, two-thirds of the world's people had an average annual gain in income of less than one dollar.[4] In 1975, according to World Bank data, nations with a total population of 1.2 billion had per capita income under $150 and reported a per capita income gain in the year of less than two dollars.

The poverty gap is, in reality, a death gap. John Darnton reported in the *New York Times* (Jan. 5, 1977) that 100 of every 1,000 Nigerian babies die before the age of five, and half that many die before the age of one. For children in Nigeria, the overall mortality rate is forty percent; for children in the United States it is three percent.

Absolute poverty has been defined by assuming that annual per capita income, based on U.S. dollars and prevailing prices in 1971, cannot sustain minimally adequate nutrition, clothing, education, shelter, and health. Data available in 1969 indicated that among 1.2 billion people in forty-four selected countries 42.5 million Latin Americans, 499.1 million Asians, and 36.6 million Africans had incomes below that level.[5]

Such privation traps humans in "an environment of squalor, hunger, and hopelessness . . . so limited by illiteracy, malnutrition, disease, high infant mortality, and low life expectancy as to deny its victims the very potential of the genes with which they were born."[6] Its result is seen in the tragic plight of Ecuadorian children who died of hunger and whose autopsies revealed stomachs filled with roots and dirt. It becomes hard reality in the fact that a child born in India has a life expectancy of forty-one years, whereas in the United States it is seventy-two years.[7]

William J. Byron, S.J., describes poverty as the "sustained deprivation of wealth (and, derivatively, deprivation of health, shelter, food, education, employment and human dignity)."[8] Poverty is maintained by social and political power, exercised in a framework of human relationships. This power resides in a combination of three factors: numbers, resources, and organization. The poor outnumber the affluent, but the affluent have resources and organization. The status of affluent and poor is reinforced by law, social custom and values, and direct or indirect control of police and military power by the affluent.

The poor unwittingly support the power that keeps them poor. In an analysis of "Patterns of Poverty in the Third World," economist Charles Elliott concludes that the system for producing and distributing goods rests on "confidence mechanisms."[9] These mechanisms function through *social and economic differentials:* access to education, health care, and employment, the ownership of property, wage rate differences, and group conflict. Because of their confidence in the system, says Elliott, the poor participate in a process that, to the physical burdens of their poverty, adds the deprival of human dignity and human rights.

Nutrition

Hunger and malnutrition can be used as a measure of poverty. According to Ruth Leger Sivard, *World Military and Social Expenditures, 1976,* the world average calories per capita was 2,520 per day, and the grams of protein, 70 per day. The average for Bangladesh was only 1,840 calories, 40 grams of protein; for Zaire, 2,060 calories, 33 grams of protein; for Guatemala, 2,130 calories, 59 grams of protein. In North America, the average was 3,260 calories, 104 grams of protein.

A 1974 UNICEF study reported that about 224 million of India's 600 million people consumed less than seventy-five percent of the calories they needed. A World Health Organization study claims that about thirty percent of sub-Saharan Africa's children do not get the needed nutrients. The result is premature death for some, and, for others, lifelong mental and physical retardation.

The poverty curtain weaves throughout the United States. In 1970, the U.S. had 5.4 percent of the world's population and 39.6 percent of the world's gross product.[10] Yet, in 1971, reports the U.S. Bureau of the Census, eleven percent of the nation's people lived below the poverty level established by the federal government. In 1975, the Bureau reports, one in five U.S. households had income below $5,000. Poverty in the U.S. is acutely skewed to age and race. Of the nation's 26.5 million poor, in 1971, fourteen million were over sixty-five or under seventeen years of age. The unemployment rate for blacks was twice that for whites. As in the rest of the world, in the U.S. the poverty gap grows wider each year. Absolute dollar differences in income have increased every year since World War II, while the incidence of poverty has remained virtually unchanged.[11]

John C. Donovan observes that the nation's "War on Poverty" failed because those whom the program was designed to benefit stood beyond the usual boundaries of United States politics. They inhabited the "other America," so they remained outside the conscience of the rest of the nation. That cut the nerve of the campaign against poverty and led to its abandonment.[12]

If the poor are to come within the concern of the affluent, we must develop an understanding of stewardship that relates humans to the resources that sustain life. For ethically sensitive persons, especially for Christians, that task is critical.

Stewardship for Our Time

Stewardship is a part of the moral life. It is what we do because of what we believe—about God, ourselves, each other, the world. It refers to the way we get and use the resources essential for the sustenance and quality of life. It is *obedient, answerable, intentional,* and *faithful.*

That "the earth is the Lord's and the fullness thereof, the world and those who dwell therein," is a fundamental article in religious belief. One corollary of such belief is *obedience* to law that has its roots in divine ownership of the earth and that limits the rights of human ownership. For ancient Hebrews, those limits were prescribed in the Law and the prophets. For us, rights of ownership and use must stringently be conditioned by human rights. A corollary of the belief that all of the world's people are the people of God is a duty to act toward every human, affluent and poor, in justice, mercy, and love.

To neglect the impoverished fourth of the world is to defy God. But the biblical testimony is that to love God is to love God's people (cf. Mt. 25 and 1 Jn. 3:4). If any of God's family is in need, to love God is to fill that need. To fill that need may require work to change the system for producing and distributing goods, if that system withholds essential goods from some of God's people.

Stewardship is *answerable.* In the belief that God is acting in all actions upon us, it responds to those actions in ways appropriate to God's action. Responsible behavior is responsive behavior—toward God, the neighbor, the earth, and oneself. Stewardship is action that anticipates answers to our answers, fully senses social solidarity, and accords with the dependence of human life upon the earth and upon God.[13]

When famine struck Judea in the first century, the apostle Paul sought contributions from Christians in the Greek city of Corinth to relieve hunger among Christians in Jerusalem. Generous help for the poor in Jerusalem, he wrote, will be your fitting response to the generosity God has shown you in Corinth. It will stir up gratitude to God in Jerusalem. It will validate your faith. It will heal the rift between Jewish and Gentile Christians. It will further unity within the Church (2 Cor. 9:1-15).

To narrow the gap between the poor and the affluent will require the skills of technicians, managers, politicians, economists, demographers, agronomists, and others. Their work, however, will depend upon the development throughout the world of a great corps of persons who have a strong ethical will to respond to the situation of the poor with empowerment: social, political, and economic. Such answerable stewardship will be particularly crucial for persons to whom such empowerment means a curtailment of their wealth and power. Frantz Fanon makes the point plain: "The question which is looming on the horizon is the need for a redistribution of wealth. Humanity must reply to this question or be shaken to pieces by it."[14]

Answerable stewardship is rooted in experience of God's goodness (roots in backward-looking reasons). In the Old Testament, the Law arises out of the claim: "I am the Lord your God, who brought you out of the land of Egypt" (Ex. 20:2). In the New Testament, the law of love arises from the claim that before we loved, we were loved (1 Jn. 4:7-11). *Intentional* stewardship is rooted in hope (roots in forward-looking reasons).[15] It senses life's openness and believes that life is not fated to be exactly what it is or will become. Life is response to opportunity, to the lure of the future. In Jesus' story of the wise and foolish virgins, the silly maidens fix their future by actions they choose and omit (Mt. 25:1-13). The story ends with a plea for watchfulness oriented to the future. In his story of the dishonest steward, Jesus commends not that servant's deceit, but his shrewd anticipation of days to come (Lk. 16:1-9).

The Bible portrays humans as called to be agents of the divine plan and, in co-creative partnership, to share God's continuing creativity.[16] God not only limits and orders our life, but creates conditions of its opportunity. "Behold, I have set before you an open door, which no one is able to shut" (Rev. 3:8). Openness and hope beckon to us from within the future.

Stewardship moves toward that future, its intention shaped by purpose and hope, its love reoriented by a proper love of God, its use of earth's resources guided by that love and hope. Stewardship sees as scandalous a world where some have too much while others are crushed by deprivation. Not fated, it believes, is a future in which this condition is permitted to grow worse. Such a future, and its consequent cataclysms, will be a judgment on our failure to use material and human resources for shaping a future that is just and humane, and thus peaceful. Stewardship views the possession of wealth not as fiefdom, nor merely as trusteeship, but especially as opportunity.

Nine Responses to World Poverty

Concern for the poor is growing throughout the world. Because the income gap is so wide and deep, the search for ways to narrow the gap is a massive enterprise. The newness of the modern contrasts of wealth and poverty means that humankind lacks an inventory of useful experience in dealing with the problems those contrasts produce. Even so, diverse approaches are being taken by many agencies at work on varied aspects of the problem.

Nine responses can be discerned, each having its own limits, some appearing to be wholly inadequate, and some offering hope.

Among the affluent, the contrast between their good fortune and others' misfortune is generating *guilt*. Guilt, however, does not relieve poverty. "Bear fruits that befit repentance" (Lk. 3:8). The demand is for effective action. But guilt may produce little more than mild malaise, or it can make us defensive, like the U.S. official who, at a news conference in Bucharest, reacted to charges that we are a nation of over-consumers with the angry claim that our foreparents came to an undeveloped continent and by hard work made it abundant, adding that if others wanted to experience similar abundance, let them work to attain it in a similar way. Guilt can end, also, in a feeling of futility as it is added to the problem that generates it.

Neither malaise, nor defensiveness, nor futility will help the poor. The best fruit of repentance is work that reveals a "turn around" in our stewardship of wealth.

Neglect is a response to world poverty—deliberate policy, as proposed by advocates of lifeboat ethics or triage, or the outcome of indifference and preoccupation with our own comfort.

Despite a general moral outrage and outcry against the proponents of lifeboat ethics and triage, our inaction in recent famines has had the effect they propose. A study by Worldwatch Research Institute reports that between 1970 and 1972 there were over two million avoidable deaths during food shortages in India and Bangladesh. Similar deaths due to hunger over the past five years have been a factor in the recent slowdown in world population growth, so much so that world population is not now expected to double by 2000 A.D.

Neglect, however, is an unfitting response to poverty. It is the response of the rich man to Lazarus, of the accursed in the story of the last judgment to the Christ who addressed them in the hunger, nakedness, sickness, and homelessness of the poor. Whatever our rationalization, neglect of poverty is likely to be motivated by our self-regarding greed.

Constraint of consumption and modification of life-style is a response of some affluent persons to the poverty of others: set the thermostat at sixty-five degrees, eat lower on the food chain, drive a small car, use mass transit, ride a bicycle, walk, air dry laundry, grow herbs for houseplants, have a garden, use a shopping bag and save paper—the list is lengthy.

For many morally sensitive people, the popular prodigality of life-styles in the U.S. and Canada is simply unacceptable. To constrain consumption of material "goods" is an attempt to avoid the folly of the rich farmer of the Gospel who responded to abundance by constructing bigger barns. An abstemious life-style offers the possibility that, from what we save by cutting down our consumption, we can create a sum to help relieve the poverty of others. Such a life-style sets prophetic witness amid prodigality. Its difficulty is that it rests on voluntarism and demands a greater moral will than many people can muster. Another difficulty, as many who constrain their consumption know well, is that it does not assure that resources not consumed by the well-off will find their way to the destitute.

Emergency *relief* through religious and secular agencies—

Church World Service, Catholic Relief Services, CARE, Lutheran World Relief, and others—is another response of compassion and good will. Its aim is simple and direct: get food to the hungry, clothes to the naked, medicine to the sick, and shelter to the homeless. The response is immediate and, when administered by such agencies as those listed above, efficient.

The relation, however, of relief given to wealth retained makes clear what Joseph Fletcher means in contrasting philanthropy, which he sees as microethical stewardship, with distributive justice, which he sees as macroethical stewardship.[17] Relief is often important and urgent, but it is only a partial and temporary solution for poverty.

Aid, granted by developed nations to nations in process of development, is a way of generating wealth at the top of an economy, on the theory that some of it will "trickle down" to the poor. Growing inequality in income, not only between, but within nations suggests that "trickle down" is a myth. Not infrequently, an elite controls the government that receives the aid and is the chief beneficiary of the wealth it generates. Moreover, "aid fatigue" appears to have brought a reduction in the percent of gross national product allocated for development assistance by such major nations as Australia, France, the United Kingdom, and the United States. U.S. aid dropped from .53 percent of GNP in 1960 to .17 percent in 1977.[18] Such economists as Montek Ahluwalia doubt that either trade or aid will be adequate to remedy third and fourth world poverty.

Trade between developed and developing nations is proposed as a response to the problem of world poverty. In 1964, the United Nations Conference on Trade and Development organized to negotiate the price and other conditions in the sale of commodities in the world market and, by similar means, to stimulate trade. The World Bank and the International Monetary Fund grant credit to developing nations on favorable terms. In other ways, they also encourage commerce between developed and developing nations.

With increased trade, however, comes the question: How can it be assured that benefits gained through improved commodity agreements will bring increase in economic benefits to poor farmers and not serve only to enrich further the brokers, managers, and merchants? Until the issue of distributive justice is resolved, neither aid nor trade will serve the needs of the poor.

In the current debate over *development* as a way of attacking world poverty, a United Nations study reports that it finds no "insurmountable barriers to an accelerated development of the developing regions of the world in the twentieth century."[19] The argument between advocates of stasis state and growth economies appears to have been settled in favor of the latter.

Not settled, however, are issues over the direction, rate, and control of growth. Mahbub ul Haq points out that a high growth rate, attained through military production or the creation of luxury goods for the privileged, may not be as desirable as a lower growth rate that is more evenly distributed. The question, he points out, is not merely how much is produced, but what is produced and how it is distributed.[20]

Development has become an important component in mission strategy among the churches. For example, in western India there is a region with rich soil but deficient in rainfall. Food had to be imported into the economically depressed region and bought out of meager incomes. Through an ecumenical consortium, a team of missioners led local farmers in obtaining well-digging and irrigating equipment, trained them in its use, helped them to form buying and marketing cooperatives, and thus to grow wheat and other food and market their produce.

While development is high on the agenda of most poor nations, it is a complex process that includes the activity of many world agencies, some private, such as foundations, some national, some international, like UNCTAD. Development raises many questions. What are "goods"? How can human values cherished by a culture be conserved at the same time that economic development takes place? How can a developing nation employ its own resources for development and avoid the hazards of relying on others? How can the fruits of development be distributed so that there is an upgrading of the condition in which the poorest forty percent of the world's people are compelled to live?

The most difficult problem in the empowerment of the poor is the problem of distributive justice. Is *consensual redistribution* possible? Will the developed nations voluntarily consent to essential transfers of economic power to developing nations? Within a nation where the annual growth rate in GNP is three or four percent, if easing the burden of poverty is to be achieved solely out of that growth margin, even if we assume that population will remain at the same level and the more affluent people in the nation will accept a stagnant income, how much inroad will be made on the burden? And can we assume a no-growth population rate in the developing nations or the willing self-assignment of the privileged to stagnant incomes?

In the search for a "new international economic order," the Seventh Special Session of the General Assembly of the United Nations, on September 19, 1975, proposed that the U.N. be restructured "so as to make it more fully capable of dealing with problems of international economic cooperation and development in a comprehensive manner." For the time, negotiation has replaced the politics of confrontation between developed and developing nations. Seven tedious and urgent issues require negotiation: (1) export earnings of developing nations; (2) international trade reforms; (3) global food programs; (4) resource transfers; (5) acceleration of development; (6) institutional restructuring to aid development; (7) the problems of the poorest countries and "absolute" poverty.

The stance of our industries and government regarding these issues will be crucial. Where issues relate to hunger, a major component of poverty, the support of such movements as Bread for the World will provide citizens an instrument for influencing public policy.

But essential transfers of power and wealth may not come voluntarily. In that case, we can anticipate their *revolutionary redistribution*. There are Christians whose judgment is that God is acting in the experience of modern China, the newly independent nations of Africa, and the revolutionary ferment in South America. They desire a more just public policy toward the poor in the United States. They support Catholic and Protestant leaders in Latin America who are harassed, jailed, exiled, or shot because they struggle for the economic liberation of the poor and for human rights. They back southern African leaders who challenge white supremacy—leaders like the black nationalist Roman Catholic

Bishop Donal F. Lamont of Rhodesia and white Afrikaner Dutch Reformed pastor Beyers Naude.

In some cases, the turmoil and violence that attend revolt will end in political liberation and the economic empowerment of the poor. In other cases, the last state of the poor may be worse than that in which they began—or equally as bad. They will simply have found new exploiters and tyrannizers.

The complete elimination of world poverty may elude us, not because we lack consensus as to broad principles and goals, or the natural resources for attaining these goals. Human affairs are complex, and human judgments, even among the ethically sensitive, differ over the means for achieving common objectives.

Moreover, in the assessment of human nature in Christian faith, all human judgments are corrupted by sin. In the struggle for justice, "we are not contending against flesh and blood, but against the principalities, against the world rulers of this present darkness" (Eph. 6:12). The seat of that contention is the human spirit. Thus, to accord justice and mercy to the poor may be too much for our moral resources.

This realism will not blunt our intention or capacity to respond. It will save us from the despair that perfectionism produces. Our aim will not be more perfection, but *faithfulness*. That faithfulness will prevent our deafness to the call to help the sister or brother trapped in poverty. It will keep us from rationalizing away the will to act.

Our faithful and fitting answer to God's call in the poverty of our sister or brother will be to respond, whoever we are, with whatever we have and whatever we can bring ourselves to do for their sustenance. It will be to join God in action that brings the poor within the concern of the affluent. It will intentionally direct the use of the earth's resources for that human liberation and fulfillment which God intends for the life of the world and those who dwell therein.

NOTES

1. Barbara Ward, *A New Creation?* (Vatican City: Pontifical Commission Justice and Peace, 1973), p. 67.

2. Lester R. Brown, *et al.*, "An Overview of World Trends," *The Futurist*, Vol. VI, No. 6 (December 1972).

3. *Monthly Bulletin of Statistics*, United Nations, July 1976, Vol. XXX, No. 7, pp. xxii-xxiii.

4. Mahbub ul Haq, "The Crisis in Development Strategies," *Anticipation*, No. 12 (September 1972), p. 3.

5. *The U.S. and World Development*, Roger D. Hansen and the Staff of the Overseas Development Council (New York: Praeger Publishers, 1976), pp. 144-145.

6. Robert S. McNamara, "World Poverty: Massive But Solvable," *A.D.*, Vol. 5, No. 5 (October 1976), p. 26.

7. *Information Please Almanac Atlas and Yearbook*, Thirty-First Edition, 1977, p. 734.

8. William J. Byron, S.J., *Toward Stewardship* (New York: Paulist Press, 1975), pp. 23f.

9. Charles Elliott, *Patterns of Poverty in the Third World* (New York: Praeger Publishers, 1975), pp. 11, 389-399.

10. Encyclopaedia Britannica *Book of the Year*, 1976: see p. 276, Table I, World Shares of Population and Production.

11. Jayne C. Millar, *Focusing on Global Poverty and Development* (Washington, D.C.: Overseas Development Council, 1974), pp. 28-29.

12. See John C. Donovan, *The Politics of Poverty* (New York: Pegasus, 1967) and Louis A. Ferman, *Evaluating the War on Poverty* (Philadelphia: The Academy of Political and Social Science, 1969).

13. For a detailed analysis of the ethics of answerability, see H. Richard Niebuhr's *The Responsible Self* (New York: Harper and Row, 1963).

14. Quoted in Byron, *op. cit.*, p. 50.

15. I am here indebted to James M. Gustafson who, in two unpublished lectures, treated the relation of stewardship to the ethics of intentionality. For a description of that ethic, see Gustafson's *Theology and Christian Ethics* (Philadelphia: Pilgrim Press, 1974), pp. 153-159.

16. See Hans-Ruedi Weber, "The Blessing of the Lord: Jewish Attitude to Material Wealth," *Laity*, No. 21 (April 1966), published by the World Council of Churches, Geneva, Switzerland.

17. Joseph Fletcher, *Moral Responsibility* (Philadelphia: Westminster Press, 1967); see Chapter XI, "Wealth and Taxation."

18. Hansen, *op. cit.*, p. 203.

19. "The Future of the World Economy," a study published by the United Nations, New York, 1976.

20. *Op. cit.*, p. 4.

Related Material for
Section II: Issues

Discussion Questions

1. How should the costs of environmental concern and stewardship of resources be fairly supported, assuming that the farmers are willing to care for these concerns if they do not bear the
   costs alone? (Geiger)

2. Can our system of economics be adjusted to allow concerns of
   stewardship of resources to enter into economic considerations? (Geiger)

3. What are some feasible and practical means of incorporating
   stewardship considerations into U.S. agricultural policy?
   (Geiger)

4. The author claims it is morally imperative to succeed in reconciling the real and apparent conflicts between producers, consumers and the hungry. Can you distinguish between "real"
   and "apparent" conflicts? (Jones)

5. Food surpluses and food reserves are often considered identical. What is the difference between the two? (Jones)

6. How is the food reserve question related to the survival of the
   family farm? (Jones)

7. The author gives four criteria for managing food reserves. Do
   you find them adequate? (Jones)

8. Should land and vital resources be privately owned? If so,
   should restrictions be placed on private ownership? In what
   way? How much land is too much? (Pignone)

9. How are ownership of land and capital and the problem of
   world hunger related? (Pignone)

10. What impact does the concentration of land ownership have on rural communities? on urban centers? (Pignone)

11. What are the long-term effects of continued reliance on fossil fuels? of the growing dependency of agricultural production on energy inputs? (Pignone)

12. How would you describe your image of a future world living in dynamic equilibrium? (Walther)

13. Can you identify and describe religious, tribal or other communities that demonstrate a great deal of stewardship in their activities? (Walther)

14. Just how compatible or incompatible do you see stewardship with a free enterprise social system like ours in the United States? (Walther)

15. If we Americans had practiced more stewardship in our natural gas system during the 1970's, what do you think would have happened in the northeast and midwest during the winter of 1977 when the weather became so abnormally cold? (Walther)

16. What changes do you think you would make in your diet or that of other Americans if stewardship were practiced more actively? (Walther)

17. Why is inaccessibility to credit a major problem for poor countries? (Land)

18. Discuss the statement, "What the south asks is only what the north professes to believe in—free markets." (Land)

19. Poor countries want a fair share in the processing of their raw materials. Who opposes this? Why? (Land)

20. Three Gospel writers attribute to Jesus the statement: "You always have the poor with you" (Mt. 26:11; Mk. 14:7; Jn. 12:8). What do you think Jesus intends in saying that? Use a commentary. Talk the question over in a group. You may particularly want to decide whether this justifies fatalism and inaction in respect to the problem of poverty. (Siudy)

21. What are the characteristics of poverty in your community? Who experiences it and why? What is done to remedy it? What

action do you consider essential for its relief? for its elimination? (Siudy)

Action Suggestions

1. Plan to talk over issues of responsible agricultural development with local farm groups or farmers and seek their opinions
of possible actions. (Geiger)

2. Look into the Community Land Trust movements in your
area. For information, contact International Independence
Institute, West Road Box 183, Ashby, Massachusetts 01431.
(Geiger)

3. Write a thirty-second radio public service spot on the need for
an international grain reserve. Try to get the spot placed on
your local radio staton. (Jones)

4. Learn about the effort of Bread for the World to get adequate
food reserve legislation in Congress. Then find out your own
senators' and representative's stands on the issue. Let them
know your view. (Jones)

5. Find out who owns the land in your county by studying the
county land books which are open and public documents.
(Pignone)

6. Determine where the property tax burden falls in your county.
Who owns the most land? Who pays the most taxes? (Pignone)

7. Organize a food buying co-op that purchases directly from
local farmers. (Pignone)

8. Study reports from the U.N. Law of the Sea Conference (most
recent session, May 1977). What stewardship principles are
present? Absent? (Walther)

9. Some municipalities use paper waste as a supplementary fuel
for generating electricity. Find out if this is the case where you
live. If not, start a discussion about the possible advantages of
the practice. (Walther)

10. Find out about the World Peace Tax Fund. Explain to at least one other person the possible relation of the fund to the debt, credit and trade demands of the south. (Land)

11. Draw up a list of basic human needs and customary human wants. Number the items in order of priority. Then make a plan for responding to "needs" and "wants." State clearly the basis for your decisions. (Land)

12. Write your own definition of stewardship. (Siudy)

Suggested Reading

Barnes, Peter. *The People's Land: A Reader on Land Reform in the United States.* Emmaus, Pennsylvania: Rodale Press, 1975.

Catholic Rural Life. Des Moines: National Catholic Rural Life Conference, Volumes 24, 25, 26. (This monthly publication consistently deals with the pertinent topics of land, energy, agriculture, hunger, and the interrelationships between these problems.)

CSPI Energy Series. Washington, D.C.: Center for Science in the Public Interest, 1973-1975. 7 Volumes.

Dubos, René. "Symbiosis Between the Earth and Humankind." *Science,* No. 193, 1976.

Eckholm, Eric. *The Other Energy Crisis: Firewood.* Washington, D.C.: Worldwatch Institute, 1975.

Eckholm, Eric, and Frank Record. *The Two Faces of Malnutrition.* Washington, D.C.: Worldwatch Institute, 1976.

Fitz, Raymond. "Organizing for Development Planning: Methodology, Models, and Communication." *International Conference on Cybernetics and Society, IEEE,* November 1976.

Grain Reserves: A Potential U.S. Food Policy Tool. Washington, D.C.: U.S. General Accounting Office, 1976.

Hayes, Denis. *Energy: The Case for Conservation.* Washington, D.C.: Worldwatch Institute, 1976.

Perella, Frederick, J. *Poverty in American Democracy: A Study of*

Social Power. Washington, D.C.: United States Catholic Conference, 1974.

Pimentel, D., D. Terhune, R. Dyson-Hudson, S. Rochereau, R. Samis, E. Smith, D. Denman, D. Reifschneider and M. Shepard. "Land Degradation: Effects on Food and Energy Resources." *Science,* No. 194, 1976.

Schumacher, E. F. *Small Is Beautiful: Economics As If People Mattered.* New York: Harper and Row, 1973.

Sewell, John W., ed. *The United States and World Development: Agenda 1977.* New York: Praeger, 1977.

Sivard, Ruth Leger. *World Military and Social Expenditures 1977.* Leesburg, Virginia, WMSE Publications, 1977.

Thomas, W. H., Jr. *Man's Role in Changing the Face of the Earth.* Chicago: University of Chicago Press, 1956.

Towards World Food Security: International Approaches to Food Stocks 1945-75. Washington, D.C.: FAO Liaison Office for North America. Reprinted from the FAO "Commodity and Review Outlook for 1974-75" by Freedom from Hunger/ Action for Development.

Trezise, Philip H. *Rebuilding Grain Reserves: Toward an International System.* Washington, D.C.: The Brookings Institution, 1976.

World Food Situation and Prospects to 1985. Washington, D.C.: U.S. Department of Agriculture Economic Research Service, No. 98, revised March 1975.

III
Responses

Parenting in a Hungry World

Patricia M. Mische

How do we help our children develop their creative potential
to respond positively in the midst of realities such as world hunger
instead of being overwhelmed by guilt or succumbing to apathy,
pity or despair?

That is the overriding question Jerry and I found ourselves
asking as we considered the ways and degree to which we should
involve our three children in our concerns about hunger and stewardship.

Guilt, apathy, pity and despair are not only of no help in
developing an adequate resolution on issues such as world hunger.
They are destructive—destructive of self and destructive of the
human community. They sap us of the will and ability to use our
energies constructively.

We certainly did not want to deluge Ann, Monica and Nicole
(who, when we began this consideration, were pre-schoolers and
are now aged 11, 10 and 9) with pictures of starving, emaciated
babies. Nor did we want to use hunger as a means to get the
proverbial spinach down. "Eat it because people elsewhere are
starving."

On the other hand, the protectionist attitude that one should
not ruin childhood by exposing children to the existence of such
unpleasant realities as hunger did not seem realistic.

Between these two extremes, there is, we are convinced, a
healthy approach of conscious, intentional parenting that helps
children develop important attitudes, values, world view, life-style
habits and some of the practical skills essential for a positive
contribution in the whole earth community.

Broad Context: A Way of Seeing and Being

To look at world hunger as parents—as family—is to look at much more than hunger. It is to assess our values, our assumptions, our way of seeing and being in the world as a family linked with other families and with the whole life chain.

It is to discover that what we believe and what we do impacts not only on ourselves, but the whole earth community, including the soil, the plants, the animals and the whole human community. It is to discover that when we touch on any one of these areas we touch on everything else.

It is in this wider context that we place our family's response to world hunger—not as an isolated issue, but as part of a holistic way of seeing and being in the world—a way of standing in relationship.

We do not do *for* the hungry. We stand in relationship *with* them. Together we share our one earth system with all life forms. There is one God of all. As the words of Christ keep reminding us, these are our brothers and sisters.

Why is Conscious Parenting Important?

If parents want their children to negotiate financial arrangements or to have the opportunity to choose a science career when they grow up, they make sure that they learn basic math skills from an early age on. Because they don't want their children to be illiterate, and because so much depends on it, they make sure that at home and at school, their children develop reading and writing skills. They encourage their physical development in Little League sports, swimming lessons and gymnastics. They stretch their aesthetic capacities in art, music, drama and dance opportunities. They send them off to camps or scouting activities to provide opportunities to experience nature. They look to their children's moral and spiritual growth.

They do all this because they are rightfully concerned about the opportunity for their children to develop all their potentialities. They want them prepared to negotiate life in the "real" world in which they will have to live.

The Real World

Yet the "real" world we parents knew as children has changed and is changing radically. Ill-prepared in our own upbringing to evaluate, choose from among viable alternatives and initiate concrete efforts in response to global concerns, we often feel at a loss to help our children develop insight and experience in this area. Yet this is the very area in which now, more than ever before, the world community is in need of prepared people. Only with deeper spiritual insight, expanded loyalties, life-reverencing values and practical skills that are all integrally developed will humankind be enabled not only to ensure its own survival but also to design a healthy future.

Reality: Over 500 million face starvation or severe malnutrition and brain damage from hunger. These are men, women and children and not statistics at issue.

Link that with the trend toward another reality. By the year 2,000 when our youngest will be 32 years old, there will be only one fourth as much arable land as there was a century ago[1] (due to erosion, strip-mining, industrial development, highways, parking lots, military destruction and other humanly caused factors). Connect that with the expectation that the world's population will double by the year 2000.

Putting these realities together adds up to not only increased hunger but also increased world tension. With a rapidly expanding armaments race that now sees humankind spending $300 billion annually on weaponry, and with increasing numbers of countries having nuclear capacity (including the availability of fissionable products from non-military nuclear reactors, as well as nuclear weapons), it is now considered probable that there will be nuclear war by 1999.[2]

The ramifications of these realities for family life in the next several decades are staggering. Our children *are* involved.

Reality: In our society, people spend millions on diet products to remove the fleshly symptoms of over-consumption. Millions more are spent on advertising that urges people to pursue the good life. The good life is imaged in terms of *having* more and more consumer goods rather than in *being* more in integral relationship with others on a finite and limited earth home. (For children this conditioning begins with their first undiscerning television experiences of a world full of Barbie dolls, G.I. Joes and Sugar Pops, without limit.)

Importance of Early Years in Family

Until very recently there has been almost no formal school or public education of any significance facilitating the growth of young people in the attitudes, experience and skills to participate in reversing the trends that breed hunger and ecocide and to help them participate with others in moving the future in a positive direction.

What little there is is often offered only as an optional high school social studies course for advanced seniors. It reaches too few and very late in their development.

We know from research in psychology and human development that the ages from birth to twelve years are the most critical. Beyond that it becomes very difficult to change behavior patterns or reverse attitudes. It is vital, therefore, that this type of education begins early and that it is part of conscious parenting.

"The world" is not something apart from the lives of our children. It is their lifeline. Every day it impacts on them and their future in a thousand ways. And every day in a thousand ways, from the baby in Pampers being conditioned to bottled baby food in one hundred sugary flavors to the teenager buying his or her first car, young people impact on the world.

Key Areas of Parenting

The following are some of the areas we consider key in conscious parenting relative to global issues such as hunger. It is not a list of ten easy steps or ten things children can *do*. There are things children can do, and this list includes reference to some. But these activities will make little sense to a child, nor will they have a significant effect on the development of a child's potential to be a creative participant in shaping human history, unless they are undertaken in a wider framework of understanding and attitudinal development.

1. Not What We Say . . .

Because children learn not by what adults say, but by what they experience, it is imperative that this conscious parenting begin in an assessment of our own parental values, assumptions, life-styles and behavior patterns.

If, in our life-styles, we participate in activities that harm the land, the water systems, and plant and animal life through our careless attitudes, pollution, over-consumption or warfare, then we rob life from our children and teach them by osmosis to rob it from their children and all the world's children.

If, on the other hand, we begin in our family life-styles to use resources more sensitively, in greater consciousness and harmony with the life-giving forces of the earth system, then we contribute not only to the well-being of our own children through their learned attitudes and behavior, but also to all with whom we and our children are connected on this earth home.

2. Who Owns the Earth? A Sense of the Sacred

One of the first assumptions that we need to question as parents is the notion of ownership. It is in assumptions about ownership that world hunger is perpetuated. It is in questioning the notion of ownership that we locate a framework within which families can move toward meaningful response.

The earth is a gift, a given. It has not been made or earned by any one person or group. No one rightfully can claim ownership of the earth or any of its parts or its resources. In all the great religions this wisdom is passed to succeeding generations. The earth does not belong to humans or to one group of humans to do with as they wish. It is always the Creator's, and it is given for the nurture and fulfillment of *all,* not for the benefit of a few.

Recall the prophecy of native American Chief Seattle, leader of the Suquamish tribe:

> How can you buy or sell the sky, the warmth of the land? If we do not own the freshness of the air and the sparkle of the water, how can you buy them? . . . This we know. The earth does not belong to man; man belongs to the earth. This we know. All things are connected like the blood which unites one family. All things are connected. Whatever befalls the earth befalls the sons of the earth. Man did not weave the web of life; he is merely a strand in it. Whatever he does to the web, he does to himself. . . . Our God is the same God. . . . This earth is precious to him, and to harm the earth is to heap contempt on its Creator.[3]

This prophecy resonates with the vision of Genesis and insight of the Wisdom literature:

> And look! I have given you the seed-bearing plants throughout the earth, and all the fruit trees for your food. And I've given all the grass and plants to the animals and birds for their food. Then God looked over all that he had made, and it was excellent in everyway. (Gen. 1:29-31)

> The Lord God placed the man in the Garden of Eden as its gardener, to tend and care for it. (Gen. 2:15)

> Do not court death by the error of your ways nor invite destruction through your own actions. Death was not God's doing. He takes no pleasure in the extinction of the living. To be—for this he created all; the world's created things have health in them. In them no fatal poison can be found. (Wis. 1:12-14).

Whether one identifies more with native American wisdom, the Judaic-Christian-Islamic vision of creation, the Hindu ethic of non-harming, or the Buddhist morality of the middle way is circumstantial. There is at the deepest core of human awareness the insight that we are called to a stance of gratitude rather than greed and exploitation. We are called to maintain the earth in a state of health rather than to contribute to its destruction. This is part of the survival instinct as well as it is spiritual wisdom. If we do not care for the earth, it will lose its capacity to provide health for us. What we do to the earth we do to ourselves, our children, and each other.

It is from the stance of gratitude and non-possessiveness that we can begin to help our children grow in stewardship attitudes— not only relative to our relationship to resources and the earth, but also as a basis for sharing with the hungry.

As a family we do not give the hungry what is *ours*. We share with them what is given for the needs of all of us.

If a family were given a pie and then one child ate it all, the other members would be upset and fighting would soon break out. If, as a family, we have more than we need, the rest is not *ours* to keep or control. It is the gift intended for the rest of our larger family.

If we can make this the basis for family "giving," whether in the form of food, clothing, money or other resources, and if we can invite our children's participation on this basis (rather than "giving up"), we contribute not only to offsetting world hunger in the long range, but also to our children's spiritual growth.

3. *Interdependence: We Are Receivers As Well As Givers*

Everything is connected with everything else. Every person is linked with others in an interdependent relationship.

Urban children seldom have an opportunity to experience their rootedness and dependence on the earth, plants and animals. The source of milk appears to be colorful wax cartons, not cows. So too the bread, wrapped in plastic, comes from stores and isn't associated with wheat ripening in rain- and sun-nurtured fields. Nor do they often see the linkages between themselves and the farmer who cared for the cows, the pastures and the wheat fields.

Suburban and rural children too seldom have an opportunity to grow in awareness of their linkages and dependence on the labors and products of the urban worker. Their clothing, too, appears to come from stores and is not associated with the factory worker who transformed cotton and other resources into faded blue jeans and prom suits and gowns.

So too, relative to the issue of hunger, unless there is careful parenting, children can fail to see their own linkages and dependence on those who may, by circumstances, be poor or hungry. Instead, efforts to conscientize them about realities such as hunger may lead to facile stereotyping of whole areas of the world or sections of a city. Instead of compassion, attitudes of superiority, ethnocentrism and contempt are learned.

Parents can help avoid this by helping children grow in awareness of the ways in which they are receivers as well as givers. Most of the foods and products in our home are there through the creativity and labor of others. The cocoa in the candy bars in the Halloween booty may have been grown and shipped by laborers in Ghana. The bananas we had at breakfast are likely to be from Honduras or other Central American countries. The oranges may have been tended and harvested by migrant workers in Florida. The sneakers on our feet may be the result of the hard work of factory workers in South Korea. Our automobile may have been made with the raw resources from ten different countries and have been made into component parts in four more countries before being assembled in Detroit or Germany and purchased by our family.

We do not only feed and care for the hungry. We are also the hungry who are fed and nurtured by the efforts of others. The hungry have no less dignity than those who are not hungry. We are all dependent on each other.

Our giving is in gratitude for what has been given us. It is part of a reciprocal experience (not to be weighed measure for measure, but in cognizance that we are all beneficiaries).

It may be an interesting table discussion from time to time to invite the family to identify where the products on the table and in the home come from—including origins in nature—and the many people who helped get them to where they are now. Then, when we make family decisions about "giving" we may want to make these connections again, examining how our "giving" may help pass some of these or similar resources on to others in a chain of giving. What we are after is deeper consciousness that the resources we "give" did not originate and are not "owned" by us, but came through a great chain of cooperative effort into our homes in the first place. We are only continuing that chain of sharing.

4. Identifying with the Need for Food and Celebration

Where is the young child whose great interest is not food? What healthy baby does not cry for it at 6:00 A.M. when you would prefer to pull the covers over your head? What toddlers don't try to climb up into forbidden areas where cookie jars seduce them? Many are the parents who have been frustrated by tots in high chairs who not only wanted to taste food, but smeared food all over their face, down the *outside* of their tummy and frosted it into their hair. The aim is a total experience of food.

What pictures in their picture books do young readers stop at the longest? You guessed it. What four-year-old doesn't beg to "help cook" and then to "lick the cookie dough from the bowl and spoon"? What is the most important ingredient at every kid's party? Right again.

Capitalizing on this interest and celebration of food, parents can invite even very young children to participate in family concerns about hunger.

Even though hunger is a serious matter, the family efforts to respond need not spread gloom. Young children want little part in negative attitudes.

One Christmas Eve, discussing the meaning of Jesus' birth and life for us, and how, as individuals and as a family, we could, in the next year, have the life and message of Christ take on deeper significance in our own lives (tieing that in with our New Year's resolutions), the dialogue began to focus on the imperative, "Feed the Hungry." Things began to get a little gloomy as one member of the family after another talked about what he or she would give up or what he or she would do, or how he or she would try to generate interest in the issue among his or her friends and the groups he or she belonged to.

Nicole, then 6, wanted none of this gloom. After considering everybody's responses and thinking for a long time, she at last blurted out with excitement, "Well, I'm not going to do any of that. I'm going to give a great big party. There will be a great long table in the back yard filled with balloons and lots of food. Everybody will be invited and there will be enough for everyone."

Although not too plausible a plan, considering our financial and space limitations, Nicole was teaching me something. Children as young as six are able to imagine and empathize with the feelings and needs of others for food and belonging. (According to Piaget's studies, most children by seven or eight can move beyond egocentrism and look at things from the perspective of another and empathize with his or her feelings.) They can understand the feelings involved in not having enough to eat or not being included in "the family" in the "group celebration."

They can image symbolically what their preferred world would be like. (For Nicole it would be a joyful banquet.) But they have little patience for the incremental and patient steps that have to be taken toward realizing goals. They want a change that is instantaneous and comprehensive. They also have little room for responses sown with guilt or morbidity. They prefer responses associated with celebration.

It certainly makes sharing a lot more fun when we adopt the spirit of Nicole's resolution. Our family responses to issues such as hunger should be positive and celebrational, because, if we think about it, there really *is* enough for everyone and everyone *is* invited.

5. *"I Can Do Something"*

We found it is important for children to discover their ability to respond in the here and now. It is no good to tell them what they can do "when they grow up."

It is also important that children be enabled to decide upon their *own* response, at their own level of readiness. They should have a voice in family decisions that affect them.

For about a year after Jerry and I made a decision to stop eating meat altogether, and even though we were careful to allow the children freedom to make their own choice on the matter, Nicole (whose calling in life is to keep her parents honest) used to remind us: "I didn't decide to be a 'veginarian.' You can still cook chicken for me."

Such a radical decision as a major shift in family diet needs the participation of all members of the family, especially because food is so important to them. But even less substantial decisions about family life style or sharing family resources with the hungry should involve the children.

Children are more likely to follow through on decisions if they helped make them. It also gives them valuable experience at creative decision-making. And, very importantly, it helps develop confidence and a positive self-concept.

If children are to develop their capacities to respond positively to issues such as hunger, they need experiences that convince them: "I can do something." "What I do now matters to other people." "I am an important part of the family and the human community. My services are needed—not later, when I'm big, but now."

These are some of the decisions relative to world hunger that our children have made in the last several years.

A. *Less or No Meat*

Monica decided to be a vegetarian. (Ann and Nicole are sometime-vegetarians and have cut down their consumption of meat.) Since Jerry and I do not eat meat and I am careful to combine grains and vegetables in ways that sufficient daily protein is available in our meals, this has not been a health hazard. On the contrary, the health of all of us has been excellent. Jerry's blood pressure and cholesterol count went down. We seldom have colds, and the flus that seem to hit everyone else in our apartment building almost always pass us by.

B. *Fasting*

When Jerry and I began fasting one day a week and sharing the money from those meals for famine relief or hunger education and efforts at food legislation, the girls wanted to do it too. I hesitated at first and then, under their persistence, permitted one meal a week—not on a school day. Now we all fast on Sunday mornings and follow it with a celebrational brunch. Monies for the morning meal are put in a container, colorfully decorated by the children and marked "Food Box" which is placed celebrationally on the center of the table.

C. Sharing Monies

The children participate in deciding where the above monies go. It is a way of familiarizing them with the work of existing groups, such as Bread for the World, Catholic Relief, Lutheran Relief, CROP, Catholic Worker, UNICEF, CARE, etc. (It is helpful for children to know that such groups exist and how they help. Their efforts are not in isolation. They can better experience themselves as part of a large network of concerned people, making concrete efforts to respond. Without this knowledge and sense of caring and concern in the human community, children would feel cause for despair.) Monies from this project are usually divided between three types of programs: (1) immediate famine relief; (2) education about hunger; (3) political change. If the group to which we are contributing is based near us, such as the Catholic Worker, the children personally go and deliver the monies and, when appropriate, meet with the persons, both staff and beneficiaries, at the receiving end.

Many are the times they have added from their own small allowances to the amount from our Sunday fasts. Their generosity is quite voluntary and sometimes overwhelming. I have to catch myself from interfering when they come with what is for them two months' income. "We don't need it," they say to allay my interference. I sit back, knowing a message has come home more deeply than I have been prepared to live it myself.

D. Hunger Walk

The two older girls, Ann and Monica, decided to join a hunger walk as the result of a talk by a CROP representative at Monica's school. They solicited sponsors who would pledge so much per mile walked—all proceeds to go to CROP for famine relief.

E. Social Protest

The children asked to join me when I participated in the final stage of the Continental Walk on Disarmament and Social Justice. It was a fine opportunity to join others, making visible their concern about upside-down national priorities where billions are available for defense while food stamp and other programs that alleviate hunger are cut back.

I consider this exercise in participatory democracy as important a learning experience for the children as anything they might have learned in school.

F. Peer Education

Ann once decided to write a composition on world hunger for her English class and then to discuss the ideas with her classmates.

G. Adopt a Grandparent

Hunger appears in many forms. The Christmas gifting that the children decided on one year was to adopt a grandparent—someone in a nursing home who had no family or friends.

The decision arose from a suggestion made by the children themselves during the news revelations of nursing home scandals. This was how they wanted to respond. We agreed to it and all of us met with representatives of a nearby nursing home. Within a few weeks we met our new grandfather whom we visited weekly until his death.

Mr. Lindau, an immigrant and professional gardener who had worked on large estates, enriched all of our lives with tips on gardening and his love of nature. The experience was also an education on the loneliness of many aged who are left in situations where they feel deserted and powerless.

Conserving and Recycling

Our family, like many we know, has always been the beneficiary of used clothing, which, if it is still wearable after being passed through three children, is passed along for even further use by others. But all are making a conscious effort to be more sensitive in our use of other resources, such as energy, and in the type of household products we use. Do those products have chemicals harmful to air, soil or water? Are items such as paper products, disposable bottles, etc. a necessary or wasteful use of resources? Although the relationship to hunger may seem remote, everything is connected. Caring about the soil and water quality is part of caring about world hunger. Now the children sometimes ask me, "Are you sure you should use this? Maybe it's not good for the earth." They have become a voice of conscience in the family. I drew the line, though, when they began carting home big shopping bags full of all the old bottles and cans that they could find tossed around our urban neighborhood. They wanted me to take them somewhere for recycling.

Later, when I thought about it, I knew I had missed an opportunity to build on their interest and look into ways of getting a recycling center in a community where now there is none.

Fred Ferber, a friend of our family's, has recently patented a way for communities to turn garbage, non-toxic wastes and mine tailings into rich top soil. With soil depletion one of the critical problems in producing adequate food, Fred's "proto-soil" is likely to contribute to long-range efforts to offset world hunger. It can be relatively cheaply produced in large quantities. "I can" attitudes such as those of Fred Ferber also need to be encouraged in our children.

There are certain to be many more possibilities for our children to develop these "I can do something" attitudes and experiences as they grow, including more sophisticated organizing skills. As their knowledge of the complexities of the problem grows and their skills broaden, they will be prepared to relate to issues such as a world food authority, grain reserves, and issues of unemployment, world trade and banking systems that vitally affect hunger patterns.

We hope that some of the experiences they are having now will provide them with the attitudes, confidence and readiness to relate themselves to these aspects of the hunger issue also.

We began including our children in our concerns about world hunger because they are vitally affected by the world and we are convinced it is important for them to develop their capacities to contribute to a positive future for themselves and the human community. We were not prepared for some of the dividends that these efforts have had. These have included deepened family life, a sense of shared commitment, a heightened sense of responsibility and confidence, a sense of belonging in the human community and a deepened sensitivity, compassion and reverence for life.

NOTES

1. According to the Environmental Quality Index, published in 1972 by the National Wildlife Federation, in collaboration with the UN Environmental Conference.

2. This prediction was made at the Harvard M.I.T. Arms Control Conference, February 1976.

3. From a speech delivered in 1854, to mark the transferral of ancesttral Indian lands to the federal government.

Stewardship and Life-Style

Jennifer Haines

A couple of years after I graduated from college, my family home burned down. I was not there at the time. My younger sister woke up in the middle of the night, smelled smoke, got everyone safely out, and in five minutes the place was an inferno. It burned to the ground.

It was the only home I had ever known. My family moved there when I was almost three, and we all worked together to build the second half of it when I was about sixteen. I got a room of my own then, put up the interior walls, painted and decorated, and accumulated happy memories there, in a sunny corner, looking out through cycles of seasons over the lawn, garden and woods. The house was full of mementos from my childhood, things I had created, things others had created for me, and treasures from past generations.

Now all these things were gone. It took me a day or two to get over the shock of it, the realization that suddenly a stable piece of my life had radically changed. Then the enduring reaction to the experience hit me: it was relief. I felt as if a great burden had fallen from my shoulders. No longer was I responsible for a lot of things that meant too much to me to give or throw away, and which I never used. I rapidly recognized that all the things important about them had never been lost because they were held in my head and in my heart. That was the beginning of my freedom to move lightly, to live anywhere, and to feel at home in all of the world.

It was also an important milestone in my personal pilgrimage toward proper stewardship of the earth, which has been inextricably intertwined with my pilgrimage toward God. Both lead joyously in the joint direction of simplicity and community.

The signpost for this pilgrimage has been the great commandments: "Thou shalt love the Lord thy God with all thy heart, and with all thy soul, and with all thy mind. This is the first and great commandment. And the second is like unto it: Thou shalt love thy neighbor as thyself" (Mt. 22:37-39).

But the more I looked to this signpost as my guide, the more clearly I saw that I was on the wrong road altogether. I was living a perfectly ordinary, quiet, moral, fairly disciplined life, in which almost all my attention and energy was given to ordinary daily details, like food and friends and dentist appointments, getting what I needed in order to do what I had set for myself, and doing it. I spent an hour every Sunday morning with God, served on church committees, and sometimes read the Bible.

And the Bible said to me, "No one can serve two masters. . . . You cannot serve God and mammon" (Mt. 6:24).

It was perfectly clear to me that I was serving mammon. There was no way that I could be loving God with all my heart and soul, as long as I was, in fact, paying very little attention to God and acting out instead my love for a great list of lesser things, like eating and managing my life efficiently and being praised for my accomplishments. I obviously needed to become detached from all that—not necessarily to eradicate it from my life, but to stop loving it, to make room for God in my soul.

So I started consciously to simplify. Losing the family home, and all the learning that came with that, was a gift that set me firmly on the road. I never accumulated such a burden of unnecessary things again. But a few years afterward, I stopped to ask myself if my possessions were again possessing me: Were they standing in the way of my hearing a call from God that would leave them behind? Were they holding me so tightly that I could not happily give them to a stranger in need? Were they erecting barriers of fear or suspicion in me against others who might damage or steal them? If so, they were walling me off from loving God. I found out how much I had enslaved myself to them by identifying, of all the things I owned, the one I most cherished, and deciding to give it away. That was a struggle. It culminated in an interiorly storm-filled worship service, where my love for God finally won. I gave the thing away. And then I knew freedom. Love for God had broken a chain of my enslavement to the world.

Over the years that have followed, each of my struggles to give up something that I was loving more than God has brought me, ultimately, to a new dimension of that freedom, God's freedom, the freedom to reach out to God and to other people in love and service because one's own wants and needs are not standing in the way, tying one down.

That freedom enables me to begin to live the second commandment: to love my neighbor as myself. I have a world full of neighbors, all of whom have needs. I cannot, of course, meet all of their needs. But I have come a long way if I can only begin to see that their needs are really as important as my own. That sounds somehow perfectly logical, but it is not the way that Western society has trained me to think or act. Our society—built on entrepreneurship, on a theoretical "balance" of power and opportunity created by everyone looking after his or her own interests, on acquisitiveness and competition and "getting ahead"— reinforces the selfishness of human nature. Together, they instill in each of us the belief that my needs naturally come first.

Such a belief is completely contrary to the Bible and all the teachings of Christianity: "Give to every one that asketh of thee; and of one that taketh away thy goods ask them not again. And as ye would that people should do to you, do ye also to them likewise" (Lk. 6:30-31). "Yet lackest thou one thing: sell all that thou hast, and distribute unto the poor, and thou shalt have treasure in heaven: and come, follow me" (Lk. 18:22). "For what is one profited, if one shall gain the whole world, and lose one's own soul?" (Mt. 16:26).

Competition and greed are not by any means even the only basis on which human societies have historically been organized. The Zuni of New Mexico are a good example of a highly cooperative society.[1] Such a society, which emphasizes meeting the needs of others and of the community, is not only a natural consequence of living Christian values; it also can be seen to work.

More than that, it seems to me that it is absolutely required by the present state of the world. We live in an age of crises, when we have hardly begun to cope with an apparent world food shortage before we are hit with an apparent shortage of oil. There is nothing imaginary about the finite limits on such natural resources. Of course, we can expect them to run out, and it will not take long at our present rates of use.[2] For future generations alone, we must find ways to use less rather than more. But it is a myth that there is not now enough to go around,[3] or that there is no way to use less without increasing the misery of the poor.

A major part of the problem is that some of us, the world's rich, have taken much more than our share.[4] Western industrial societies encourage each one to take as much as he or she can get. You and I are among those who are depriving others by using more than we need of all sorts of limited natural resources. In fact, we have gotten so used to expecting to have more than we need that it is hard for us to realize that many of the things we call "needs" are actually luxuries. And the world cannot afford such luxuries.[5]

One of the exciting dimensions of my own pilgrimage has been freeing myself of personal "needs." With my metabolism, for instance, I do not need three meals a day; someone who does should get my third one. But habit was so strong in me that it actually took years of fighting a tendency to gain weight before I discovered such a simple fact. I tested myself on the need for a car one year when I lived in the country five miles from work; I found that cycling or walking was not only an adequate alternative, but also much more healthful and enjoyable.

I recognize that this kind of decision would be much harder to make if I lived twenty miles from the nearest bus and had three small children. But I must never forget that that is the situation of millions and millions of poor people, who are our neighbors, whom we should be loving as we love ourselves. Do I need a car, in such a circumstance, more than they do? How can I possibly justify taking such a large chunk of the world's resources and leaving them so little? Perhaps there is a better way to provide for the needs of all of us.

This, I think, is what stewardship is all about. "The earth is the Lord's, and the fullness thereof" (Ps. 24:1), and all of us on earth are the Lord's stewards. Our job is to care and use God's resources, as God would do. Absolutely nothing that we "own" or "acquire" is ours. It is God's, given freely to us, for our use. (Here, too, we could learn from native American peoples, who cannot even imagine "owning" the land.[6]) God has promised to provide for our needs (see Mt. 6:25-34). The earth has enough to supply the needs of all its people. So we must see to it that God's riches are properly shared: "For I mean not that other people be eased, and ye burdened: But by an equality, that now at this time your abundance may be a supply for their want, that their abundance also may be a supply for your want: that there may be equality" (2 Cor. 8:13-14).

In a sense, the task is easy, because we, the affluent, have the solution to the problem in our hands. We have the excess. All we have to do is to stop holding on to it and find good ways to get it to those who have the deficit. The second part of this solution is admittedly very tricky. It undoubtedly requires an extensive reworking of the international economic system, based on a new set of assumptions about how people should interact with each other. Christianity could offer much in providing the assumptions.

But the letting go must happen before anything can be redistributed, and though it is obviously required, it is still very difficult to do. It is hard for us really to believe that all we own is God's, that if we give up material security, God is security enough (see Mt. 6:19-21), and even that all the world's people are our neighbors (see Lk. 10:29-37). "And seek not ye what ye shall eat, or what ye shall drink, neither be ye of doubtful mind. For all these things do the nations of the world seek after: and your Father knoweth that ye have need of these things. But rather seek ye the Kingdom of God; and all these things shall be added unto you. Fear not, little flock; for it is your Father's good pleasure to give you the Kingdom" (Lk. 12:29-32). We read these truths in the Bible, and they are so contrary to our worldly experience that they often fail to sink in at all. We need to keep struggling with them, and with the details of our daily lives, freeing ourselves to love God and neighbor more, to simplify, to release resources for others. This, as I see it, is the first stewardship task of the Church.

This task involves us immediately in community. Community is the body of Christ, the Church, the fellowship in which we worship God; it is also the fellowship in which we find support to make the difficult changes in our lives that lead us away from the world's ways and into God's ways. "Be not conformed to this world," said Paul (Rom. 12:2), "For that which is highly esteemed among people is abomination in the sight of God" (Lk. 16:15). When we obey, the world raises its eyebrows (or worse), and we do not cringe, because our brothers and sisters in Christ support us. Further, the security of trusting a loving, sharing community is a major step along the way from trusting material things to trusting God.

Community is also more. Community is a large part of the practical solution to stewardship questions. When I talk about getting rid of things in my life, people often object, "But you can't get rid of *every*thing. You have to eat, don't you? You have to have protection against the winter cold. You have to draw the line *some*where." I agree. I do need the use of a few things, such as some clothes and blankets. There are some simple tools that radically enhance our capacity to do various jobs, which I like to have available. But I do not need to own any of them. Just as in the early Church, where "all that believed were together, and had all things common, and sold their possessions and goods, and parted them to all, as everyone had need" (Acts 2:44-45), the things that I use can be owned by the community and used by many people. Alternatively, they could be privately owned and extensively shared.

This strikes me as both a personal and a societal solution to problems of resource use. It frees me from the possessiveness of private ownership without depriving me of the use of necessities. At the same time, it employs efficiently many products embodying scarce resources, which would otherwise sit around idle much of the time, or which would be used at only a fraction of their capacity. A good example is the private automobile which is often used by one person at a time.

Of course, we need societal alternatives to these wasteful patterns, such as adequate mass transit. We need a reawakening of Christian values which emphasize the responsibility of each of us for the care of the common goods for the good of all. We need to relearn conservation, for the benefit of both present and future generations. We need to create the world system which can best translate our saving and sharing into available resources for the use of others. We must work for all of these things. All are part of the stewardship responsibility of the Church.

At the same time, we can make a start in our own lives through Christian community, giving away many of our goods and sharing the rest. This can be done even without stepping out of nuclear family situations. We can share washing machines and automobiles, child care and home repair. The more simply we live, the less we need to earn to support ourselves and our families, so we can spend less time working for money and more in serving others. Or, one or more members of a group can stop earning altogether in order to serve full-time.

This notion of service is one that we must beware of romanticizing. We may like to imagine ourselves on some distant frontier, bringing life to a starving family. But service is usually both much closer to home and much harder than that. Service is loving our neighbor. This includes seeing that our neighbors' needs are as important as our own, and giving up for them things that we may want for ourselves. It also includes recognizing that we are not great dispensers of largesse around the world, but learners; that our poor neighbors have as much to give us as we may have to give them; that, in fact, they deserve, as a right, the power over their own lives, and their share of the earth's bounty, which the rich have denied them. When we, the rich, have satisfied our basic stewardship responsibilities, have met the requirements of justice, and are no longer wealthy at the expense of the poor, then, I think, we can afford to give and serve simply in "charity," which is love.

I was rather surprised to discover not long ago that the gross global product per capita (that is, the average share of the world's wealth each year for each person) is not much less than $1,000.[7] Some people have estimated that, with ideal management, the earth could support its entire population at a level near $2,000 each.[8] Recognizing the obvious inadequacies of such measures and estimates, I still find grounds in these figures for a great deal of hope, for they are attainable. Even in the United States, there is nothing terribly visionary about $2,000 a year per person (or $8,000 for a family of four). I see it as a realistic yardstick, at least as a beginning, in the effort to simplify our personal lives materially.

I have been living on approximately $2,000 a year for the past couple of years and loving it. What makes it easy is being part of an intentional community, with Quaker roots, called the Philadelphia

Life Center. Its members are active in a non-violent social change network called Movement for a New Society. We live in cooperative households of seven to ten people, in a residential area of the city proper. Every adult supports himself or herself usually by working about half-time. That frees time and energy for reaching out to other people and working for social change.

House members share food buying and cooking, household maintenance, chores and child care. The households generally do not pool income entirely, but that is an option. We spend $7-10 per person per week on food. That includes largely vegetarian cooking and quite a bit of quantity buying, as well as growing and preserving some of our own produce. Very often, one person in a household has a car, which gets shared around. Philadelphia has good public transportation, and many of us have bicycles. None of us has central air conditioning. Few have television or large pets. We create most of our own recreation, especially by simply having fun with each other.

This leads to a very full and joyful life. Many of the things that save both money and scarce resources do take time, and I have been delighted to learn that that time is rewarding in itself. Walking is the best example I know in my own life. I walk about four miles home from my job, which takes about twice as long as the trolley. It is my only regular exercise, and a built-in time of mental relaxation, which I need particularly at the end of an office day. It is also a wonderful opportunity to interact with God's natural world, even in the city, and it opens me up to worship. It is a great gift.

This kind of life, particularly for church people concerned for global stewardship, has been expressed by one group of Christians[9] in a pledge called "Toward a Church of the Beatitudes":

Recognizing that Christ's Gospel of love, liberation, justice and peace is either promoted or obscured by the life-style and manner of exercising power in Christian communities and gatherings,

And that Christ calls his people to a spirit of profound repentance and love, to put apathy behind, and to participate fully in the on-going responsibility of God's loving community,

We pledge ourselves to accept God's claim on our personal and corporate lives and to encourage our Church communities in these directions:

1. To be poor in fact, adopting new and radically simpler life-styles, refusing to increase our affluence until all other persons and human communities have essentials.

2. To be poor in spirit, renouncing identification with worldly wealth and power, thus nurturing our obedience to the spirit of the living Gospel.

3. To preach, teach and practice Gospel simplicity within our Church institutions, urging the Church to use its resources to bring justice to the hungry, poor and oppressed.

4. To develop cooperative and participative patterns of living, sharing, working and relating.

5. To take up Christ's role of humble service and gentle love in leadership and decision-making, and to resist abusive power relationships.

6. To work for ending racism, sexism and age and class discrimination in our Church communities, so that through loving and non-violent action the Church can effectively contribute to healing these sins in the world.

7. To proclaim prophetically the need for a just world distribution of power, wealth and natural resources.

8. To accept the cross, and the joys and pain of discipleship, ready even to be persecuted for justice.

The cross and its liberation mark all of my own journey toward simplicity. Each step forward is a tremendous struggle, and finally a new step into freedom and joy. It is a new step toward God. Whatever my simplicity does for the world, it benefits me immeasurably, and I know that it benefits the world as well. I might be amazed at how neatly one simple solution answers many problems, but I am convinced that this is God's way, and I am not surprised that God's solution is perfect.

NOTES

1. Margaret Mead (ed.), *Cooperation and Competition among Primitive Peoples,* rev. ed. (Beacon Press, 1961), pp. 313ff.
2. Donella Meadows, *et al., The Limits to Growth* (Universe Books, 1972), pp. 55ff. See also Hans Landsberg *et al., Resources in America's Future* (Johns Hopkins Press, 1963).
3. For example, see Meadows *et al., op. cit.,* pp. 163-167.
4. For example, see Georg Borgstrom, *Too Many* (Collier, 1971); Frances Moore Lappe, *Diet for a Small Planet,* rev. ed. (Ballantine, 1975); Ronald Sider, *Rich Christians in an Age of Hunger* (Inter-Varsity Christian Fellowship, 1977).
5. E. F. Schumacher, *Small Is Beautiful* (Harper and Row, 1973), especially pp. 21-31.
6. Margaret Mead, *The Changing Culture of an Indian Tribe* (Capricorn Books, 1932), p. 38.
7. I calculated this two years ago from Lester Brown's statement in *World Without Borders* (Random House, 1972, p. 211) that the gross global product is nearly $3 trillion. Using more precise population figures (3.7 billion in 1971), I get a figure closer to $800.
8. For example, Meadows *et al., op. cit.,* p. 165, arrived at a level of $1,800.
9. Campaign for Global Justice, 4709 Windsor, Philadelphia, Pa. 19143 (1976).

Stewardship Community—
A Fantasy

George E. Knab, O.M.I.

It was a homily on stewardship that proved to be the catalyst for Tom and Nancy Wilson in their thoughts about the future. Unfolding the meaning of Jesus' parable of the talents, the priest made a striking application. "The money we think is ours," he explained, "is really God's gift to us. He welcomes us to spend on ourselves what we need. The rest," he went on to say, "we are to invest in the divine treasury which is the poor. St. Augustine said, 'He who has a surplus possesses the goods of another.'"

Tom's fingers interlocked Nancy's. They looked at each other; enthusiasm seemed to leap from their eyes. For the past year they had wrestled within themselves, between each other, and among several friends over the possiblities of a more responsible, more Christian, way of life. What they heard, especially the quote from Augustine, came as a release; somehow the pieces of their vision were falling into place.

Relationships

A process of re-evaluation began in earnest for the Wilsons eighteen months earlier, in a marriage encounter weekend. This was a program designed to help a couple enrich their marriage relationship through a practice of interpersonal communication. When the weekend was over their four children noticed a change in their parents. Tom and Nancy were beginning to savor the wonder of their love at a deeper level of awareness, and their behavior was showing it. Soon they were helping their children to unfold, and all took delight in the experience. What the two of them had valued so much before—a fine home, a spacious backyard, the new den Tom had built—all seemed to pale in significance as they discovered how much more their marriage and family relationships had to offer.

Father, Brother, and Inner Life

Two months after their marriage encounter weekend Tom and Nancy were persuaded by friends to attend a charismatic prayer meeting. Here they were encouraged to participate in the "Life in the Spirit" seminar which led to baptism in the Holy Spirit. Soon their faith, which had been a somewhat vague awareness of the ultimate meaning of life, unfolded to become an experience of a personal relationship with God. They learned that God is a Father who cares for them; in Jesus he is brother and Savior, and through the Holy Spirit he is their inner life as well. The same profoundly personal meaning they were discovering within their marriage relationship now was beginning to color their relationship with God.

Trust

It was at a day of renewal for all charismatic prayer groups in the city that Tom and Nancy experienced their maturing faith as a challenge to their life-style. "Many people say that God helps those who help themselves," said the guest speaker, a local Lutheran pastor, "but this is a damnable half-truth. The gospel truth is that God helps those who hope in him." The pastor commented on how few believers give God a chance to provide for them. "Instead of living day-by-day with trust in his promises," he said "we squirrel away our material blessings and place our trust in them." Nancy thought of their investment in real estate, and Tom recalled his insistence on an expensive life insurance policy. "Let's begin to depend more on what God will provide," the pastor encouraged, "and less on what money can buy; then we'll know how good it feels to have God for our Father."

The speaker concluded with several examples of how God did

indeed provide for those who trusted in him. The stories were hard to believe, and Tom and Nancy went home confused.

Stewardship

Shortly after the day of renewal, the Wilsons' parish began a Lenten series of talks and discussion. The focus of the series was stewardship. Tom decided to go. He started learning at the very beginning when the opening speaker challenged his concept of ownership. "In the Book of Leviticus," Tom was told, "God says, 'The land is mine and you are but aliens who have become my tenants'" (Lev. 25:23). The speaker interpreted this to mean that ownership is proper only to God. "What is proper to man," he said, "is stewardship; it is our responsibility to administer what we have according to the will of God who is the only true owner."

"And what is the will of God?" Tom thought to himself. The answer quickly surfaced: "God wants us to share what we have so that everyone will have enough. Like the sun, the rain and the air we breathe, the earth and its fruits, in fact everything money can buy, is meant for all. Private property and personal earnings are only the means by which we are called upon by God to manage a portion of creation for the benefit of all." The speaker continued his assault on Tom's pre-conceptions with a quote from St. John Chrysostom: "The rich are in possession of the goods of the poor even if they have acquired them honestly or inherited them legally. When we refuse to give and to share, we deserve to be punished as thieves."

America the Beautiful

In a subsequent session of the Lenten series the stewardship of the United States was examined. The statistics that were introduced were hardly complimentary: Americans who compose six percent of the world's population consume forty percent of its resources; only .5 percent of America's personal income goes to charity, and less than .2 percent of the nation's GNP is spent on foreign aid. "And *Look* magazine in one of its final issues," a participant in the discussion interjected, "projected that in the middle 1970's Americans would be spending $250 billion annually trying to have fun."

That, everyone agreed, was hardly good stewardship. "America has adopted *Better Homes and Gardens* as her scripture," another participant commented, "Madison Avenue is her preacher, and 'Keep up with the Jones' is her golden rule; and that is not very good for the rest of the world."

Tom had been in the service during the Korean War, and he always got defensive when people criticized the United States. "I believe that America is the greatest country in the world," he insisted, "and we can thank God for everything we have. But I'm learning that we can be even greater, and that is by sharing, really sharing our blessings with others. Then America the great can become America the beautiful." The pause that followed Tom's heartfelt call was interrupted by someone who inserted another remark attributed to Mother Teresa of Calcutta, "If people in the United States do not answer the needs of the people, they will miss the touch of Christ in their lives. What is given to them is given to share, not to keep."

The Richest Ten Percent

As Tom shared with Nancy the substance of the discussions, both became more aware of a call to make a more complete personal commitment. "What can we as a family do in order to know the touch of Christ in our lives?" they asked each other. Tom was making about $15,000 a year as a real estate broker, and someone told him that those who make over $12,000 a year are in the richest ten percent of the world's population. "Maybe God is providing me with this chance to make $15,000 a year," Tom reflected, "so that we can share four or five thousand of it with some of the other ninety percent."

"But Tom," his wife objected, "with prices the way they are today, we need all the income we're getting just to make ends meet."

Tom was not going to be put off by Nancy's pleas for realism. Instead he persuaded her to play a little game. "Suppose our family budget," he suggested, "was based on an income of $10,000 a year, how would we live?" As they let their imaginations run their course, they found themselves moving into a less expensive neighborhood, selling their second car, reducing the amount of meat in their menu, cutting back on insurance, giving up their investments in real estate, and trusting that their children would find enough money to pay for their education after high school. They discovered that if they really wanted to, they and their children could enjoy a good life on two-thirds of what Tom was making that year.

"What would we do with the rest?" Nancy asked.

"Well, if I knew of a man in the poorest ten percent of the human race," Tom mused, "who like myself had a wife and children to support, and if four or five thousand dollars of my money would be enough to help him have and hold a job by which he could provide a decent life for his family, I'd give it to him." Nancy did not challenge her husband's dream as she marveled how much his attitude and her own had changed. Just two years before they thought they had found their niche in the American middle-class suburban environment. Now they were talking of a house in the city, less meat on the table, and getting by with only what they really needed.

The Wilsons were ripe for the words that came from the pulpit that Sunday morning in September: "He who has a surplus possesses the goods of another." Now was the time to move from words and ideas to action.

Community

For several months a number of people in the charismatic prayer groups of the city had been talking about forming community. The early Christian community described in the New Testament (Acts 2:44-47 and 4:32-35) fascinated several couples who mused among themselves about what form such a community would take in contemporary America. Tom and Nancy realized that their goal of being good stewards could not be achieved in isolation. Only the support of a community and the pooling of resources could make it viable. They decided to invite ten very interested couples to a meeting at their home. The first meeting led to several meetings, in the course of which the life and structure of a community emerged. Different couples emphasized different values. Prayer, common worship, social action, interpersonal growth, personal freedom, and family integrity were all included. Tom's emphasis was stewardship. "Let's live as simply as possible," he encouraged. "Let's keep for ourselves only what we really need and share everything else with those who need it more." He supported his point with a text from Scripture, "We brought nothing into the world and certainly we can take nothing out; but having food and sufficient clothing, with these let us be content" (1 Tim. 6:7-8). Responses to Tom's remarks generated a name for the group. They called themselves the Daily Bread Community. They would trust in God for what they needed day by day, and what was left they would give away.

Moving Out

Having made a personal commitment to the Lord and to each other, the members of the emerging community took some decisive steps. They realized that the spirit of this commitment was paramount, but they realized that some very specific life-style changes had to be made to lend substance to their ideals. The first concerned a place to live—everyone would move. Physical transplantation would help them part from the old and begin the new. The second was a pledge to adopt a significantly less expensive style of living; each family committed itself to live on seventy-five percent of its total income.

Urban Environment

As they looked for an environment in which to relocate, their attention focussed on a neighborhood on the near east side of the city. This was once a middle-class residential area that had deteriorated over the past twenty years as many of its citizens moved to the suburbs. Because the population was transient and integrated, new households could move in without attracting too much attention. One value they saw in the east side neighborhood was the opportunity to live in physical proximity to each other. A few homes within walking distance of each other were already on the market, and Tom learned that probably others would be available soon. A church and school were in the area, and this was considered a great advantage. The neighborhood was serviced by a couple of bus lines which gave the community access to the business and cultural districts of the city. A second car would cease to be a practical necessity for any family.

Eight of the ten families owned their own homes scattered in various suburbs of the metropolitan area. It was decided that as houses were available, each family would sell their own home and use the money to buy a house in the east side neighborhood and to do whatever repair and remodeling work was necessary. The rest of the money would be invested in U.S. savings bonds to provide a financial resource in case the family decided to withdraw from the community. Two of the houses would be doubles in order to serve those members of the community who preferred to rent. Moving from their pleasant home in the north side suburb was a painful experience to Nancy. As she packed she thought of the work and the excitement that had been theirs as she and Tom made their house just right for the family—a kitchen picture window overlooking their backyard, a playroom and a workroom in the cellar, the den of course, and in the living room some new shelving to accommodate a stereo system and the trophies their children were starting to collect. But it was at her insistence that Tom bought a two-family house. "If relationships are more important than things," Nancy argued, "then let's make sure we have more relationships in our new home."

In the Midst of the Poor

Another value the Daily Bread Community saw in their new

neighborhood was an opportunity to be in dynamic relationship with the poor. Some of their new neighbors were elderly people, others were women with small children living on welfare, and many were families with low incomes who saw in the neighborhood their first chance to own their own home. The community did not perceive themselves, nor did they want to be perceived by others, as do-gooders; they simply wanted to be good neighbors. When this matter was discussed, Tom shared a quote he read of Mother Teresa. "The poor are great people," she said. "They give to you much more than you give to them." The community concluded that their relationships to their neighbors would be natural; what they would share would be themselves rather than their ideas or their things. "Let's offer them our time, our interest, and our willingness to listen and learn," Tom insisted. "Then let's offer anything else that comes naturally."

The Twenty-Five Percent

A central issue to the Daily Bread Community was money. "God blessed America," Tom said, "so that Americans can be a blessing to others." The ten families chose to adopt simpler lifestyles primarily so that at least twenty-five percent of what they earned could be shared. On the basis of their present earnings this would total $40,000 a year. As Tom described it, "This is now our annual surplus, and because it is our surplus, it is not really ours. It belongs to those who need it more than we do. God has given us stewardship over it," he continued, "and he trusts that we will manage it well."

The handling of money, all agreed, is a very delicate matter. As they discussed this issue they came to some unexpected conclusions. First, they would never spend any of this twenty-five percent on one another. If any family fell on hard times, they would try to help that family in every way possible without the use of money. Likewise, if a neighbor or someone in the wider community came to them in need, they would never use money as a response. Nancy declared: "I don't want money and decisions about money to be a factor in my relationships with the people I meet, no matter what is their need. I'd rather let the providence of God and the creativity of our own Christian love suggest alternatives."

The community decided that their money would go to people beyond their environment. In fact they believed it should go beyond the borders of the United States. "In this country we have the best-situated poor people in the world," someone commented, "and there are a lot of agencies already trying to help them. Let's use our money where people are really poor."

"But let's use it in a place which we can easily visit," Tom encouraged, "so we can see how it will be spent."

Helping the Poor Help Themselves

With the desire for oversight came a call for caution. "I don't want our money to run other people's lives," Nancy said. "I think the money we give should help other people run their own lives." Acknowledging the validity of this viewpoint the group decided to devote their annual surplus to funding a program designed to help the poor help themselves.

After a great deal of investigation they settled on a program in Mexico administered by the Federation of Associations for Social and Educational Assistance (FASE). Originating in Brazil this organization had proven itself effective in helping communities identify needs and mobilize resources. With the support of the state government, FASE focused its methodology on a very poor district in the Yucatan Peninsula. The surplus from the Daily Bread Community would supply half of the funding; the other half was provided by funds raised among Mexican themselves. This money was needed to support the organizers, give scholarships to some of the children, establish a craft cooperative, and make available low-interest loans for agricultural equipment. The FASE people committed themselves to send monthly reports and to welcome a couple from the Daily Bread Community who planned to visit and study the program first-hand.

Full-Time Jobs?

As the community realized the possibility of finding satisfaction through more simple life-styles, one of the members questioned the value of full-time jobs. One of the men, an electrical engineer, commented: "Considering all the time, study, energy, and experience I've devoted toward developing the skills of my own profession, I think good stewardship suggests that I continue working in my field. In fact," he continued, "I even see my position as a call to bring Christ into a circle of associates who need a relationship with him as much as any other group. And ever since I began 'brown-bagging' it for lunch, people have been asking questions I never had to answer before." Tom was glad to hear this comment, and he added his own observation. "Perhaps in some cases a part-time job may be considered sufficient," he said, "but it is full-time salaries that enable us to be all the more generous in support of programs that help the really poor."

Jesus, the Bread of Life

Mindful that the Daily Bread Community was the result of religious inspiration, its members were of one accord that it could be sustained only by the same. To nourish their spiritual life they all pledged themselves to be involved in the worship, educational programs and social activities of the local parish. They regularly attended the Thursday night charismatic prayer meetings at the church, and they found great encouragement in knowing that all the charismatic groups in the city were praying for the success of their community. In fact several members of these groups were already wanting to join.

Each Tuesday evening the community held its weekly meeting

to explore and decide those issues that served the common interest. The meeting was usually preceded by a home Mass celebrated by their parish priest. It seemed that their community celebration of the Eucharist was the most energizing of all their activities. "Sharing in Jesus, the bread of life," as one person expressed it, "continually inspires me to be bread for the lives of others."

Stewardship Unfolding

Within the weekly meetings of the Daily Bread Community other opportunities for stewardship began to unfold. One man commented, "I never realized how much I missed working in my backyard until I moved here." Others expressed disappointment that the homes in the neighborhood were on small lots. Noting that there was a public park nearby, they made arrangements with the city to spend a couple of hours each week working together with their children to keep it clean and trim. The park proved to be their gathering place of choice for their outdoor activities.

A plan for cooperative child care was developed at another meeting, and this brought mothers welcome opportunities to involve themselves in activities that suited their interests. And a practice of taking turns inviting other families over for supper was beginning to emerge. Several parents took responsibility for the parish program of religious education for high school students.

Experiencing the support of the Daily Bread Community, and invigorated by their own spiritual life, some members were considering even bolder decisions. Tom and Nancy were discussing the possibility of discontinuing their life and medical insurance. "I believe that if something should ever happen to any one of us," Nancy claimed, "we would somehow find the help we needed. Why spend so much each year for emergencies that may never come when other people need financial help right now in order to survive?" Tom concurred, "We're going to let the Lord provide our coverage."

Another family was making arrangements with the state probation department to use their home as a halfway house for one or two women released on parole. And a couple whose children were in their teens were considering becoming foster parents for a couple of children who were moderately retarded.

Perhaps no more fitting words can be found to close these reflections than those of Archbishop Helder Camara: "If one dreams alone, it is only a dream. If many have the dream it is the beginning of reality."

Related Material for
Section III: Responses

Discussion Questions

1. Does your personal life-style satisfy your Christian convictions? Describe some of your family's practices that represent good stewardship. (Haines)

2. What is the relationship for you between faith and life-style? Between stewardship and life-style? Between world hunger and life-style? (Haines)

3. What are some of the steps between personal simplicity and meeting world needs? What other things might also have to change to give life-style changes an effective global impact? (Haines)

4. What is the present level of awareness and world view of the members of your family? Where does this need broadening and deepening? What experiences would nourish this growth? What resources in your community could help to develop in them a sensitivity to global concerns? (Mische)

5. Consider your children and/or children you teach or work with. What are their special interests, talents and concerns? In what way can you help them channel and develop these in ways that foster their own growth and at the same time help offset and prevent local and world hunger? What community groups or resources can help you? (Mische)

6. "He who has a surplus possesses the goods of another." In what way are these words of St. Augustine true today? (Knab)

7. Can relationships supply the happiness many people find in things? (Knab)

8. "God helps those who help themselves" vs. "God helps those who hope in him." Can the two statements be reconciled? (Knab)

9. How would you live on three-quarters of your income? (Knab)

10. Why do so few Christians in America adopt the sparing-caring-sharing life-style of the early Christians as described in the New Testament? (Knab)

Action Suggestions

1. See if there are ways in which you can simplify your life. You might want to share car or tools with neighbors, try walking everywhere within two miles of your house, make your own music and celebrations, find alternatives to television, campers, motorboats, etc. (Haines)

2. Hold a vegetarian meal, a frugal meal or a fast, and contribute the money saved to relief or development work in poor nations. (Haines)

3. Discuss any changes you make with your family and wider community. Talk over problems and challenges. Discuss how your personal changes relate to the questions of economic and political justice in the world. (Haines)

4. Take about ninety minutes with your family or a group of friends to do the following exercise:

    a. What do you anticipate the world will be like in the year 2000? Consider such spheres as: family life-styles; housing, neighborhoods and cities; political and legal systems; violence, war and peace; food, land, water and other vital resources; employment; business; technology; moral and ethical codes; dominant social values.

    b. Then, for the same areas, consider what you would *prefer* the world to be like in the year 2000.

    c. Compare differences between your two scenarios. Consider what (1) awareness, (2) attitudes and values, (3) in-

sight and knowledge, and (4) practical skills members of the
world community need to move from your anticipated
world to your preferred world.

    d. Brainstorm about which experiences we can provide in our
families now that will help our children contribute cre-
atively to the development of that preferred world.

    e. From the above, choose those experiences you will per-
sonally work on in your family. Set a time and plan for
proceeding to your goals. (Mische)

5. In a family brainstorming session, list the ways your family
benefits from and depends on the work, creativity and gifts of
others. What products, food, art work, music, etc., have come
to your family through the work of others? In what ways can
your family share their work, time, resources, talents and gifts
with others in a spirit of gratitude? Choose one or more to
begin with and develop your plan of action for sharing.
(Mische)

6. The purpose of this fantasy is to stimulate responses in the
reader that may lead to life-style changes. Responses may be
noted in the margin of your text as follows:

    ? = More information needed
    X = Can't be done
    * = Shouldn't be done
    − = Good but frightening
    + = Good and exciting

Compare and explain your responses in a discussion group.
(Knab)

Suggested Reading

Arnold, Eberhard. *The Early Christians: After the Death of the
Apostles*. Rifton, New York: The Plough Publishing House,
1970.
Chapman, Paul, ed. *Clusters*. Greensboro, North Carolina: Alternatives, 1975.

Gish, Arthur G. *Beyond the Rat Race*. New Canaan, Conn.: Keats
Publishing, Inc., 1973.

Gowan, S., G. Lakey, W. Moyer, and R. Taylor. *Moving Toward a
New Society*. Philadelphia: Movement for a New Society,
1976. (More information available from MNS, 4722 Baltimore
Ave., Philadelphia, Pa. 19143.)

Jackson, Dave and Neta. *Living Together in a World Falling Apart*.
Carol Stream, Illinois: Creation House, 1974.

Shakertown Pledge Group/Simple Living Network. *Lifestyle: A
Reflection/Action Workbook*. Minneapolis: Shakertown
Pledge Group. (More information available from the Shaker-
town Pledge Group, West 44th Street at York Avenue S,
Minneapolis, Minn. 55410.)

Simple Living Program of the AFSC. *Taking Charge: A Process
Packet for Simple Living: Personal and Social Change*. San
Francisco: revised 1975. (More information available from
AFSC, 2160 Lake Street, San Francisco, Cal. 94121.)

Ward, Barbara and Rene Dubos. *Only One Earth: The Care and
Maintenance of a Small Planet*. London: Deutsch and Har-
mondsworth: Penguin, 1972.

Biographical Notes

RONALD J. SIDER, a graduate of Waterloo Lutheran University (BA) and Yale (B.D., Ph.D.), is Associate Professor of History and Religion at Messiah College (Philadelphia Campus). He served as Chairperson for three years of Evangelicals for Social Action. He is a member of the Social Action Commission of the National Association of Evangelicals and convenor of the unit on Ethics and Society of the Theological Commission of the World Evangelical Fellowship. He recently published *Rich Christians in an Age of Hunger: A Biblical Study* (Inter-Varsity Press, 1977). He lives in Philadelphia with his wife Arbutus and three children.

WILLARD M. SWARTLEY is currently Professor of Biblical Studies at Eastern Mennonite College, Harrisonburg, Virginia. He received his Ph.D. from Princeton Theological Seminary in 1973. An ordained minister, he pastored a Mennonite Church in Elkhart, Indiana from 1961 to 1965. He has recently been appointed to the faculty of the Associated Mennonite Seminaries, Elkhart, Indiana, to begin teaching in the fall of 1978.

WILLIAM J. BYRON, S.J., author of *Toward Stewardship: An Interim Ethic of Poverty, Pollution and Power* (Paulist Press, 1977), is President of the University of Scranton. He also serves as President of the Bread for the World Educational Fund.

HOWARD RICHARDS coordinates the Peace and Conflict Studies program at Earlham College, and serves as a consultant to the Center for Research and Development in Education (CIDE) in Santiago, Chile. He has been a fellow of the Center for the Study of Democratic Institutions and a volunteer lawyer for Cesar Chavez.

DORIS DONNELLY, Ph.D. has served as Chairperson of the

211

Theology Department of Immaculate Heart College in Los Angeles and director of the graduate program in Spirituality at Fordham, and is currently in seminary education in New York and New Jersey.

CHARLES K. WILBER, Ph.D. is presently professor and chairman of the Department of Economics at the University of Notre Dame, and has taught at Multnomah College in Oregon, the Catholic University of Puerto Rico, Trinity College in Washington, D.C., and American University in Washington, D.C. He has worked for the Peace Corps and the Interamerican Development Bank and has lectured before the Agency for International Development and Foreign Service Institute. Since 1969 he has been an Adjunct Senior Staff Associate at the AFL-CIO Labor Studies Center. He is author of *The Soviet Model and Underdeveloped Countries* and *The Political Economy of Development and Underdevelopment* and is working on a book with Professor Kenneth Jameson on the present crises in the American economy.

DONALD GEIGER, S.M. is Program Director of Strategies for Responsible Development, a development education and applied technical development organization at the University of Dayton. SRD is engaged in cooperative efforts with networks of groups to help further distributive justice. He is also Professor of Biology at the university, working on plant productivity research. Part of his activity includes work with normative planning to incorporate stewardship concerns into agricultural development.

PHILIP LAND, S.J., of the Oregon Province, is well known among Jesuits. After his doctorate and graduate studies in economic development at St. Louis and Columbus Universities, he worked for many years at the Institute for Social Order in St. Louis. He was professor of economics and social studies at the Gregorian University in Rome before undertaking responsibilities as senior staff researcher for the Pontifical Commission on Justice and Peace at the Vatican. He also was a leading figure in SODEPAX, the joint Vatican-World Council of Churches' committee on society, development and peace (in Geneva). He has published widely on social justice and global development. Recently he returned to the U.S. to become staff associate at Center of Concern in Washington.

MARGARET MARY PIGNONE, S.N.D. is Director of the Office of Community Development in the Diocese of Wheeling-Charleston. Her work entails community development organizing in the central Appalachian counties of southern West Virginia. She is also a member of the board of directors of the National Catholic Rural Life Conference.

BRENNON JONES is Staff Associate with Bread for the World working on policy and issue interpretation. He served from 1969 to 1971 in South Vietnam as a photographer-journalist for Church World Service covering agricultural, medical and refugee relief work in that country. He has done broadcast research for CBS on Indochina affairs. During the late 1960's he worked on low-income housing development with black community groups in Harlem. More recently he worked on the film *Hearts and Minds,* which is about the effects of the Vietnam war on America and Vietnam. He also is a consultant on hunger to the United Church Board for Homeland Ministries, and serves on the Steering Committee of the Interreligious Taskforce on U.S. Food Policy in Washington, D.C.

ERIC G. WALTHER is manager of the Food Production/Climate Mission, Charles F. Kettering Foundation. He is responsible for the development of new crop/environment models and food/climate policy information. He holds a Ph.D. in Atmospheric Science from the State University of New York at Albany.

GEORGE S. SIUDY is Secretary for Stewardship for the Stewardship Council of the United Church of Christ. He also serves as pastor of St. Peter's U.C.C. Church, Chester Springs, Pennsylvania. He holds a M.Div. degree from Drew University in Madison, New Jersey. In 1972 he was a non-governmental organization delegate to the United Nations Conference on the Human Environment, Stockholm; in 1974 he was an NGO delegate to the U.N. Conference on World Population, Bucharest. He is a member of the U.C.C. Taskforce on Ecojustice and Lifestyle and of the International Secretariat for Science-Theology Dialogue.

PATRICIA M. MISCHE and her husband Jerry are the parents of Ann, Monica, and Nicole. In the sense that her article is a result of their combined family experience and search, they all share in its authorship. Jerry and Pat are co-founders of Global Education Associates and co-authors of *Toward a Human World Order: Beyond the National Security Straightjacket* (Paulist Press, 1976). They are also adjunct faculty members at Seton Hall University. Pat has taught in African and U.S. schools and is currently working on a book for teachers and parents about developing justice, peace and global perspectives with young children.

JENNIFER HAINES lives in the Philadelphia Life Center, where she is a member of the Churchmouse Collective. Churchmouse, which is part of the non-violent social change network called Movement for a New Society, is a group of Christians working with church people for simplified personal and institutional lifestyles and global justice. She is a Quaker, a member of New York Yearly Meeting of Friends. She staffs, part-time, the Right Sharing of World Resources program of the Friends World Committee, primarily doing educational work on international development and life-style issues. She received her B.A. from Swarthmore College and her M.A. from Bank Street College of Education. She has experience as an elementary school teacher.

GEORGE E. KNAB, O.M.I. holds an M.A. in theology from Oblate College, Washington, D.C. He has served as a parish priest, and as a director of religious services in a high school. Currently he is a Catholic chaplain at the Indiana University Hospitals, Indianapolis.

MARY EVELYN JEGEN, S.N.D. Executive Director of Bread for the World Educational Fund, received her Ph.D. in history from St. Louis University in 1967. From 1967 to 1971 she taught at the University of Dayton. The next three years she spent in teaching and research in Europe and India, returning to the United States to work in the field of education on issues of justice and peace.

BRUNO V. MANNO, S.M. has his Ph.D. in Interdisciplinary Studies from Boston College where he worked under their Institute for the Study of Religious Education and Service. He is presently Assistant Professor in the Department of Religious Studies and Director of the Office for Moral and Religious Education at the University of Dayton. He lectures widely to adult audiences on topics related to value development and moral education.

The Office for Moral and Religious Education (MORES) cooperates with various community and national agencies in the joint planning and sponsorship of continuing education programs in the related areas of value, moral and religious education. Though primarily directed to adults, these programs are open to all interested parties. MORES is funded through the Contributed Services Fund of the Society of Mary (Marianists) of the University of Dayton.

BREAD FOR THE WORLD EDUCATIONAL FUND

Bread for the World Educational Fund is an educational service on hunger and related issues. It was founded by Bread for the World, an interdemoninational movement of Christian citizens who advocate government policies that address the basic causes of hunger.

Bread for the World Educational Fund does not engage in lobbying. It designs and conducts programs in collaboration with colleges, seminaries, church groups, and others. It reaches a larger audience through publication of educational materials.

Bread for the World Educational Fund
4600 N. Kilpatrick Avenue
Chicago, IL 60630
(312) 736-2218